A Bestiary of Monsters in Greek Mythology

Spyros Syropoulos

ARCHAEOPRESS ARCHAEOLOGY

Archaeopress Publishing Ltd
First and Second Floor
13-14 Market Square
Bicester
OX26 6AD, UK

ISBN 978 1 78491 950 4
ISBN 978 1 78491 951 1 (e-Pdf)

© Archaeopress and S Syropoulos 2018

All rights reserved. No part of this book may be reproduced, or transmitted, in any form or by any means, electronic, mechanical, photocopying or otherwise, without the prior written permission of the copyright owners.

This book is available direct from Archaeopress or from our website www.archaeopress.com

Contents

Preface v
Abbreviations vi
Introduction, by Richard Buxton vii
Introduction 1

Chapter 1 Humanoid Monsters 9
  Arimaspians (Ἀριμασποί) 9
  Blemmyae (Βλέμμυαι) 11
  Cyclopes (Κύκλωπες) 13
  Cynocephaloi and Akephaloi (Κυνοκέφαλοι & Ἀκέφαλοι) 17
  Giants (Γίγαντες) 20
  Phorcids (Graeae, Gorgons & Sirens) – Φόρκυς (Γραῖαι, Γοργόνες, Σειρῆνες) 27
    Graeae (Γραῖαι) 28
    Gorgons (Γοργόνες) 34

Chapter 2 Serpentine Creatures 39
  Amphisbaena (Ἀμφίσβαινα) 39
  Cychreus (Κυχρεύς) 42
  Typhon (Τυφών) 44
  Python (Πύθων) 49
  Hydra of Lerna (Λερναία Ὕδρα) 52

Chapter 3 Partly Human 60
  Centaurs (Κένταυροι) 60
  Echidna (Ἔχιδνα) 70
  Scylla (Σκύλλα) 73
  Sphinx (Σφιγξ) 78

Chapter 4 Monstrous Animals 84
  Cerberus (Κέρβερος) 84
  Orthus (Ὄρθος) 92
  Mares of Diomedes (Διομήδου Ἵπποι) 95
  Lion of Nemea (Λέων Νεμέας) 98
  Phoenix (Φοίνιξ) 103
  Hippalectryon (Ἱππαλεκτρύων) 105

i

Chapter 5 Ghosts and Daemons 109
   Eidola (Εἴδωλα) 109
   Empousa (Ἔμπουσα) 122
   Eurynomus (Ευρύνομος) 124
   Gello (Γελλώ) 125
   Lamia (Λάμια) 125
   Mormo-Mormolyce (Μορμώ-Μορμολύκη) 126
   Telchines (Τελχίνες) 127
   Epilogue 130

Works Cited 132
   Greek 137
   Ancient Greek Sources – Translations and Commentaries (English) 137
   Ancient Greek Sources – Translations and Commentaries (Greek) 138
   Electronic Sources 138
   Encyclopedias 139
   Disclaimer 139

And since mythical narrations with monsters do not cause only pleasure, but they also cause fear, the use of both of these genres is useful both for children and for adults; for we offer the delightful myths to children in order to urge them towards good, the scary ones in order to avert them from evildoing.

Strabo, *Geographica* 1.2.8.20-24

Preface

This book takes its origin from material I have been using for many years during my *Greek Mythology* courses for the program *Paideia* (a collaboration between the University of the Aegean and the Center for Hellenic Studies Paideia at the University of Rhode Island) during the past eleven years. Students have always expressed special interest in the concept of monstrosity in Greek mythology and they were always keen on details about the sources of the stories. Questions about the monsters mentioned in myths came up during classes at the University of the Aegean, in the *Greek Philology* classes, and in the classes about *Ancient Greek Theater*, at the Open University. Often people wondered about the development of a story. Which was our oldest source? For how long have people been interested in the story? How has it changed over time? I tried to answer these questions, by referring to some examples borrowed from the countless stories about monsters found in myths. I am thankful to all of these students for their enthusiastic response to these stories.

The support of students, friends and colleagues who read the manuscript of this book at various stages was invaluable. I am much obliged to Ms Vicky Hatzipetrou, who read the whole manuscript many times while it was being written and saved me from various linguistic mistakes. The same goes to Anastasios Chamouzas and Stephanie Conley, Lander University Teaching Fellow, for carefully reading chapters 4 and 5 and making amendments and suggestions I am thankful also to my students Shelby Wood, Shauna Bailie Fletcher, Amber Ramirez, Carver Rapp and Ciara Barrick, for reading various parts of the manuscript. My good friends John Harding and Jonathan Leech took precious time of work and holidays to read parts of the book. Special thanks to my former student Anastasios Mavroudis (now Father Zacharias) for his meticulous reading and corrections. Finally, I am indebted to Prof. Mercedes Aguirre and Prof. Richard Buxton for their support over the years, and their willingness to read the whole manuscript so carefully, make amendments and suggestions that informed its final form. Thanks go as well to Marianna Nikolaou who read the final version of the manuscript and made the final corrections

Finally, I want to thank Daniel and Stelios, my sons, who understood why long hours had to be spent in the company of text-books piled on the floor around my desk and not with them. This book is dedicated to them.

Spyros Syropoulos

Abbreviations

The abbreviations of the academic journals used in this work follow the catalogue found in *L'Année philologique*, LXVII: année 1996, Paris 1998.

AAHG	Anzeiger für die Altertumswissenschaft, hrsg. von der Österreichischen Humanistischen Gesellshaft.
AAN	Atti della Academia di Scienze morali e politiche della Società nazionale di Scienze.
AC	L'Antiquité Classique
Aevum (Ant)	Aevum Antiquum
AJA	American Journal of Archaeology
AJPh	American Journal of Philology
BICS	Bulletin of the Institute of Classical Studies of the University of London
CJ	The Classical Journal
ClAnt	Classical Antiquity
CPh	Classical Philology
CQ	Classical Quarterly
CR	Classical Review
CW	The Classical World
GRBS	Greek, Roman, and Byzantine Studies
HSPh	Harvard Studies in Classical Philology
JHI	Journal of the History of Ideas
JHS	Journal of Hellenic Studies
JNES	Journal of Near Eastern Studies
LIMC	*Lexicon Iconographicum Mythologiae Classicae*, Artemis & Winkler Verlag (Zürich, München, Düsseldorf), Vol. IV: Eros (in Etruria) - Herakles (1988), Vol. V: Herakles - Kenchrias (1990).
PP	La Parola del Passato
QS	Quaderni di Storia
REG	Revue des Études Grecques
RhM	Rhenisches Museum
SCO	Studi Classici e Orientali
TAPhA	Transactions and Proceedings of the American Philological Association
WS	Wiener Studien
YCIS	Yale Classical Studies
ZPE	Zeitschrift für Papyrologie und Epigraphik

Introduction, by Richard Buxton

Monsters will always be with us. The most unpleasant one I ever met used to inhabit my nightmares when I was a boy and an adolescent. It lived in the small room at the foot of the stairs in my parents' house, where visitors used to leave their coats. The room contained some cupboards and a wooden chest. It was in that chest that the monster lived. By day the little room was insignificant; we rarely had occasion to go into it. But in my dreams, it was the lair from which the monster emerged, slowly climbing the stairs until it reached the bedroom in which I was sleeping. Unable to bear the apprehension, I would awake with a cry of terror just as it entered the room.

Like many of the best monsters, this one had no shape; or, if it did, I didn't know what its shape was. By contrast, many of the most modern monsters – those depicted in contemporary cinema – are evoked, through the use of the latest computer-generated graphics, in the most vivid and ultra-realistic detail. But of course everything changes. Just as the development of photography spurred artists into abandoning realistic representation in favour of new ways of envisioning the world – Impressionism, Expressionism, Surrealism – so it may be that the next generation of cinematic monsters will return to the shadows, remaining implicit and indistinct, creatures of a chiaroscuro underworld.

Every culture possesses its own *imaginaire*, within which monsters occupy an appropriate space. Academic study of these diverse monstrosities has progressed apace in recent decades, thanks for example to the work on 'monster theory' associated with J. J. Cohen. But alongside the theory there is room also for the painstaking setting-out of data, culture by culture, context by context, author by author. It is this latter field of endeavour to which the present work belongs.

Dr Syropoulos writes, not for the professional myth-specialist, but for readers in search of an engaging, lively and readable account of ancient Greek monsters. His style, unpretentious and often colloquial, would be at home in the classroom, where the ability to hold an audience's attention is at a premium. But Dr Syropoulos does not 'talk down' to his audience. His account of monster myths is brimful of detail, always attentive to the minute differences between the narratives of different authors. In an age where some students' first (or only) reaction to being asked a question about a myth is to Google the relevant mythological name and to reproduce the Wikipedia entry on it, it is all the more vital to have available alternative sources of information, in which a picture both more complicated and more faithful may be found.

I don't, though, want to create the impression that Dr Syropoulos' book consists of nothing but 'data'. Along the way he also makes some important general points about monstrosity. For instance, he is quite right to stress that monstrosity and ugliness are two different things: the winged horse Pegasus is 'monstrous', but certainly not ugly. A monster is something which goes against a norm, rather than going against 'nature' (p.5). Another eminently sensible observation is the following: 'Imagination is applied to create a world of transgression from the ordinary, which is coherent and immediate because it is formed with ordinary elements, only messed about, exaggerated or distorted' (p.6). This is Lévi-Strauss's idea of the myth-teller as *bricoleur*, combined with the idea that myths *refract* reality rather than *reflecting* it.

Monsters, I began by saying, will always be with us. As we walk through the unnerving forest of Greek monstrosity, Dr Syropoulos is a genial, reassuring and well-informed guide to have beside us.

Richard Buxton
February 2015

Introduction

Greek myths are enchanting. There is no denying the power of enchantment in stories that hover between the real and the fictitious, the plausible and the supernatural. Narrated, recorded, drawn, sculpted or even performed, the complex world of Greek mythology has survived for thousands of years and remains popular and contemporary in cultures other than the one that gave birth to it. To venture a convincing explanation regarding the reasons for this power of Greek myths is hard, because it would have to begin with the difficult subject of their nature.

As a matter of fact the degree of truthfulness of Greek myths is a question that posed problems even to Greeks in antiquity. 'Aristotle does not doubt the historicity of Theseus; he sees in him the founder of Athenian democracy (*Constitution of Athens* 41.2) and reduces to verisimilitude the myth of the Athenian children deported to Crete and delivered to the Minotaur(*Constitution of the Bottiaeans*, cited by Plutarch, *Life of Theseus* 16.2) As for the Minotaur, more than four centuries before Pausanias the historian Philochorus also reduced him to verisimilitude; he claimed to have found a tradition (he does not specify whether it is oral or transcribed) among the Cretans according to which these children were not devoured by the Minotaur but were given as prizes to the victors in a gymnastics competition; this contest was won by a cruel and very vigorous man named Taurus (cited by Plutarch 16.1). Since this Taurus commanded the army of Minos, he was really the Taurus of Minos: Minotaur'.[1] The first substantially recorded doubts about the 'truth' of myths are found in the works of Hecataeus of Miletus (c. 550-476 BC). Hecataeus recognized that oral history is untrustworthy and that myth as oral tradition certainly cannot claim factuality.[2] This trend was called *pragmatism*. Similar trends were adopted by Hellenistic philosophers, especially Euhemerus (330-260 BC) who rationalized mythology as history and gave his name to this method of rationalizing.[3]

It is hard to say when Greeks stopped believing in their myths. How revered is the patron deity of theatre, the god Dionysus, when he appears as a ridiculous

---

[1] Veyne (1988) 133-134.
[2] According to Shotwell (1939, p. 172-3) it was Hecataeus' visits to Egypt that influenced his skepticism, since they proved feeble his claim that he was a descendant of a god through sixteen generations. The priests showed him a number of statues in the temple, each one of them dedicated by a temple priest of each past generation. These generations amounted to 345. Thus, the gods of 16 generations before Hecataeus could not have existed. Cf. Bury (1958) 14, 48.
[3] For example, Euhemerus argued that Zeus was a king who died in Crete, thus giving birth to stories that connected him with the island. Cf. Spyridakis (1968) 337-340.

coward in Aristophanes' *Frogs*? Is he the same Dionysus whose epiphany in the *Bacchae* of Euripides proves his divinity beyond any doubt and in the most ruthless manner? What about the Trojan War? As a paradigm of past bravery, it is mentioned in many an Athenian public oration or diplomatic speech, but did the Athenians actually believe in Scylla and Charybdis, or the man-eating Cyclops Polyphemus? It seems that these old stories are so deeply embedded in the cultural consciousness of the Greeks that no one needs to scrutinize them. They are just there; and the essence of these myths is that they represent a collective memory of a non-temporal, non-chronological past, which is not doubted and thus bears the validity of history. In his book *Did the Greeks Believe in their Myths*, Paul Veyne (1988) wrote that 'imagination is a faculty, but in the Kantian sense of the word. It is transcendental; it creates our world instead of providing the leavening or being the demon. However – and this would make any Kantian worthy of the name faint with horror – this transcendence is historical; for cultures succeed one another, and each one is different. Men do not find the truth; they create it, as they create their history. And the two in turn offer a good return'.[4]

Mythology is about many things. There are always many ways to interpret what Kirk (1975)[5] defined as *traditional stories* – stressing in this concentrated definition the *tradition*, which is the most imposing medium and power that preserves and perpetuates these *stories*, the origin of which is lost in time. Even if they are not written in a canonical book, traditions have the weight and effect of legislation. They are observed, obeyed and respected without this meaning that one ought necessarily to believe in them. Many traditions contemporary to the 5th c. B.C., for example, were explained via myths – such as the tradition of sacrifice, arranged by

---

[4] Veyne (1988) xii.
[5] Kirk, Geoffrey, The Nature of Greek Myths, 1975. Besides this wonderful book, the reader may find a vast collection of many influential works on the interpretation of myths. To name but a few: Buxton, Richard, G.A., Imaginary Greece, Cambridge 1994; Cameron, Alan, Greek Mythography in the Roman World, OUP USA 2004;Doniger, Wendy, The Implied Spider. Politics and Theology in Myth, Columbia University Press, 2011; Dowden, Ken, The Uses of Greek Mythology, Routledge, London 1992, 2005 (second edition); Gantz, T., Early Greek Myth: A Guide to Literary and Artistic Sources, Johns Hopkins University Press, 1996; Guthrie, W. K. C., The Greeks and their Gods, Beacon Press, Boston 2001, first edition in 1950; Versnel, H. S., Inconsistencies in Greek and Roman Religion: Transition and Reversal in Myth and Ritual (Studies in Greek and Roman Religion, v. 6) Brill, 1993; Woodard, Roger (ed.), The Cambridge Companion to Greek Mythology, Cambridge 2007; Καρακάντζα, Ε. Δ., Αρχαίοι Ελληνικοί Μύθοι. Ο θεωρητικός λόγος του 20ου αιώνα για τη φύση και την ερμηνεία τους, Μεταίχμιο 2004.

the creator of mankind, Prometheus, as a medium of communication between the world of gods and the world of mortals.[6]

The world also needed an explanation. How was it created? How did the order of gods and other deities come into existence? Mythology comes to the aid of the pre-scientific mind and offers plausible and often amusing explanations about origins. The eruption of the universe out of Chaos, the creation of beings out of two opposites, the Sky and the Earth, is described in various *cosmogonies* and *theogonies* around the 8th c. B.C by many different poets.

Politics is another concept associated with mythology. The way that these traditional narratives were extensively used to serve specific political needs is often confirmed by tangible sources, such as the Chronicle of Lindos or the Parian Marble. These are sources that rely on local mythical history, in order to explain contemporary politics.[7] Greek historiography abounds in examples of references to myth for political purposes. Herodotus (5.79-80) describes the episode of a Theban mission to the island of Aegina, requesting an alliance against the Athenians, basing their claim on common ancestry, since, according to myth, Thebes and Aegina were both daughters of the river Asopus. Again in Herodotus, the argument of both Athenians and Tegeans over who will lead the prestigious left of the army is based on the mythical past of each city (Herodotus, I, 26-28). Beginning with their first founder, ancient cities constituted genealogies which were usually attributed and dedicated to a god, or a hero, or an offspring of a mixed marriage with a mortal. The etiological myths revealed and narrated the foundation of the city. Thus, serving the need of the community for a specific and distinct political identity, as well as, providing each city with a means for its own personality. The founder would be a moral person, a member with full rights in this first community of the city. In this sense, the etiological myth is a political ideology, while the mythical credentials of the city were used as assurance of its dynamic relations with other cities.

During an interview with one of the most influential modern scholars on Greek myth, Joseph Campbell, Tom Collins asked him about the purposes of myth. Campbell answered:

---

[6] Let us remember that a myth (from the Greek *mythos*) was not perceived as imaginary or false, as most of us would use the word today. Ken Dowden draws attention to Homer, Iliad 6. 381-2, where a servant replies to Hector's questions about his wife's whereabouts: 'Hector, since you really tell me to mytheisthai the truth'. 'The woman proceeds to give an account, as asked – this is her mythos, a worked out string of ideas expressed in sentences'. Dowden (2005) 3.
[7] Cf. Jacoby (1949) esp. pp. 147ff and 213ff. For myths used politically in tragedy see Carter (2007) 90-142.

'There are four of them. One's mystical. One's cosmological: the whole universe as we now understand it becomes, as it were, a revelation of the mystery dimension. The third is sociological, taking care of the society that exists. But we don't know what this society is, it's changed so fast. Good God! In the past 40 years there have been such transformations in mores that it's impossible to talk about them. Finally, there's the pedagogical one of guiding an individual through the inevitables of a lifetime. But even that's become impossible because we don't know what the inevitables of a lifetime are any more. They change from moment to moment.

Formerly, there were only a limited number of careers open to a male, and for the female it was normal to be a mother or a nun or something like that. Now, the panorama of possibilities and possible lives and how they change from decade to decade has made it impossible to mythologize. The individual is just going in raw. It's like open field running in football – there are no rules. You have to watch everything all the way down the line. All you can learn is what your own inward life is, and try to stay loyal to that.'[8]

Approached from so many different angles mythology is definitely multi-prismatic and it plays different roles in different circumstances. Religious or cosmological, political or entertaining, these stories explain aspects of the world that cannot easily be rationalized, or they are too prominent to be left without being put to good –political – use.

The complex world of these myths, which is often chaotic, disorderly and unsystematically recorded in conflicting versions from time to time and place to place, saves a special place for one of the Greek's most celebrated values: balance. There's no Sky without Earth. There's no Olympus without the Underworld. It's all about balance. Greek myths abound in images of beauty and perfection: charming gods, attractive goddesses, and handsome heroes, all of them standards of flawlessness, physical and spiritual. However, the ancient Greeks were not fond of absolutes. No god or hero is shown without blemishes in character and ethics and even amongst them some are far from perfect, like Hephaestus, who is ugly and lame. Another element that dominates Greek mythology is the idea of balance. Good and evil, light and darkness, hubris and punishment. What could not be missing from this world is the image of reversed beauty: monstrosity.[9] The aim

---

[8] 'Mythic Reflections. Thoughts on myth, spirit and our times'. An interview with Joseph Campbell, by Tom Collins. One of the articles in The New Story (IC#12). Winter 1985/86, p. 52. Copyright (c)1986, 1997 by Context Institute

[9] The only extant collection of essays focusing exclusively on monstrosity remains the work of Farkas, A. E., Harper, P. O. & Harrison, E. B. (eds.), Monsters and Demons in the Ancient and Medieval Worlds: Papers Presented in Honour of Edith Porada, Mainz am Rhein, von Zabern, 1987.

of this book is to explore the realm of the imaginary world of Greek mythology and present the reader with a categorization of monstrosity, referring to some of the most noted examples in each category.

Monstrosity should not be confused with ugliness. Although in modern thought the meaning of the word is associated with the abominable or the hideous, it is not the same with the mythical traditions of the Greeks. Monstrous is whatever does not resemble the usual, the common form. It is not about the unnatural. After all, what is *natural*? Natural is what is usual or common in different places and different times. One ought to be cautious of the use of such terms when one deals with Greek mythology. Even the Greeks are careful when categorizing monstrosity; in most cases they are aware of the fact that many of the Greek monsters, at least, are children of Gaea or other gods and goddesses, the same gods and goddesses who bore men and women. This makes *monsters* part of the physical world, just as men and women are part of this world, and as such they are part of the stories of men throughout the centuries.

Genealogy may be one of the revealing characteristics of monstrosity. 'Monsters are nearly always the product of a liaison which is itself abnormal. Centaurs are the offspring of a union between the rash Ixion, would-be lover of Hera, and a cloud fabricated by Zeus. When the father of the gods shed his seed on the ground while asleep, the result was a monstrous creature called Agdistis, endowed with both male and female genitals.[10] Not surprisingly, unions between monsters generate that which is abnormal: Echidna and Typhon had a most remarkable brood, including the Hydra and Kerberos.[11] Such logic is a function of the fact that a major feature of the symbolism of mythological genealogies is the expression of relationship'.[12]

I mentioned beauty as the least useful factor to define monstrosity. Beauty is not only in the eye of the beholder, but it is a value that transcends familiar forms. A man can recognize beauty in other members of his own species, but he can also define a deer, or a cat, or a horse as *beautiful*. Beauty is, thus, the epitome of idealized characteristics of each specific form at the utmost level. Subsequently, the absence of the perfect or idealized characteristics – usually socially and culturally implanted as standards of recognition – constitutes monstrosity. If beauty is the culmination of idealized standards, monstrosity is the ultimate deviation from these standards. Even this does not suffice to define monstrosity for the Greeks, who love to prove how permeable limits and definitions are in general. For example, the beautiful winged horse, Pegasus, is as much a monster (he is, after

---

[10] Pausanias, 7.17.5.
[11] Hesiod, Theogony, 306ff.
[12] Buxton (1996) 207.

all, born of the decapitated Medusa, alongside with the Giant Chrysaor), as the next 'ugly' creature, let us say the one-eyed Cyclops Polyphemus in the *Odyssey*. It does not matter whether you have an extra pair of wings or one eye less than usual. If your form transgresses the standards of its kind, then you are a monster. As Richard Buxton put it, 'a monster is chaotic, conforming to no existing class. As the case of the benevolent Centaur Cheiron shows, monsters are not necessarily characterized by the savage violence of a Minotaur or a Medusa. But a monster is always by definition an outsider'.[13]

If one observes all the monsters of Greek imagination closely, one concludes that there is not one single monster that does not bear at least one singular recognizable characteristic, which refers to some real form in nature. The human mind is not able to invent something that is not a derivative of human experience. Thus, a centaur may be monstrous, but he is half *man;* an animal can be monstrous, just because it is bigger than usual or it has some unusual characteristic (like the lion of Nemea with the arrow-proof hide); a ghost or a daemon can be monstrous, because it is full of unnatural characteristics, but it *looks* like a man or a woman in form. In order to create monsters, Greek mythology can combine forms, or distort forms but it cannot invent forms. Imagination is applied to create a world of transgression from the ordinary, which is coherent and immediate because it is formed with ordinary elements, only messed about, exaggerated or distorted.

To present the reader with a complete collection of all monsters of Greek mythology would be impossible. Over twenty seven monsters make an appearance in this book and the list is far from complete. Rather, the aim of this book is to present the audience with a categorization of monstrosity and the presentation of the most prominent creatures within each category. Thus, the creatures that enrich Greek myths and traditions from the opposite side of beauty and perfection are divided into five chapters: *Humanoid Monsters, Serpentine Creatures, Partly human, Monstrous Animals* and *Ghosts and Daemons*. Emphasis will be given to the views that come from antiquity, taking into account modern scholarship on these categories. The reader should be presented with a round, coherent narrative about each one of these creatures, using sources from different periods of history, by indicating the chronological difference of these sources, so that the evolution of the myth can be traced at least up to a point of its most recent chronological version.

In passages written or translated by others, I have maintained the grammar and spelling chosen by the original author(s). Otherwise, I have opted for the popular name: Hercules instead of Herakles, or Athene instead of Athenā, for example.

The order in which the monsters of each category are presented in each chapter is alphabetical. Creatures described by writers from different historical periods and

---

[13] Buxton (1996) 205.

different literary sources (i.e. epic, historiography, drama) appear in one category; the reader will easily trace the sources which are sometimes singular (i.e. some of the most fabulous creatures are described by Aelian only once), or have survived only in the works of later writers (i.e. the works of Ctesias, or of Aristeas)[14].

This brings me to the issue of chronological limits. To borrow the wording of Richard Buxton, 'the earliest examples of mythological narrative to which I refer are from the eighth century B.C., to which Homer and Hesiod may reasonably be dated. Deciding how further back in time to go is more difficult. The poets Oppian and Nonnos are recognizably composing in the same tradition as their predecessors of a thousand years earlier; and Pausanias' writing in the second century AD, is the richest single literary source for Greek ritual and many of its accompanying stories. I shall frequently refer to this later material, but it cannot be denied that the world had greatly changed by the time Pausanias decided to present the Greeks themselves as an object of curiosity'.[15]

This kind of curiosity culminated in a unique genre called *Bestiary*. A bestiary or *bestiarium vocabulum* is a kind of illustrated encyclopedia of various unusual entities, from animals and birds to rocks. A moral lesson is usually added to each description. The oldest collection of this kind is dated back to the second c. A.D., a Greek text by an unknown Alexandrian author.[16] It is entitled *Physiologus* and it was translated into Latin around 700 A.D. and then into many other European and Middle-Eastern languages. The Phoenix, which is reborn from its own ashes, and the Pelican, which feeds her young with her own blood are two examples of the entries that became popularized as ecclesiastical symbols.

Popularization is not exactly the aim of this book; it certainly addresses not the expert, but people who are already – and, who aren't remotely – familiar with Greek Mythology. The non-specialist will enjoy the coherent account of the myth's evolution and appreciate the changes and additions to the given myth over the years; more demanding readers will benefit from the reference to sources, ancient and modern, that will guide them further in the exploration of these accounts.

Finally, the aim of the book is not to decipher these myths. It is true that some monsters can be more plausibly explained than others. The nine-headed Hydra of Lerna, with its foul breath and toxic, poisonous blood, definitely stands for the swamps of that area – swamps that were a place of illnesses and death; people had tried to convert these swamps into good, arable land, so much needed for the agricultural Mycenaean economy. Even Hercules himself started a similar task

---

[14] Bolton (1962); Sulmirsk (1970).
[15] Buxton (1996) 6.
[16] White (1954/60). Scott (1998) 430ff, suggested a later date, around the end of the 3rd c. A.D. or even the beginning of the 4th c. A.D.

that was completed half way through the 19th century: a task so much needed to boost the agricultural economy of an impoverished Greece that had just gained its independence from the Ottoman Empire. As for the Cyclops, I am ready to accept that the myth was born when an early farmer unearthed a massive elephant skull with his plough.[17] A look at a massive rib-cage and a skull with one single hole at the place where the eyes should have been, sufficed to create stories about monstrous creatures. This single hole, which is the opening for the elephant's trunk, gave birth to the Cyclopes. One may accept such explanations and be fascinated by them. However, the aim of this book is to show how fascinating the imaginary world of these monsters is. It is not a world different from that of our ancestors. These monsters shared the adventures of ancient gods, heroes and ordinary people of Greece; therefore they will not be decoded, deciphered or explained. They deserve to be presented simply as part of this unique past of Greece, which makes it so appealing to most of us today. After all, as I often say to my students regarding Greek Mythology, *if it's not fun, it's not functional.*

Spyros Syropoulos

---

[17] Skeletons of dwarf elephants (around 1,5-2,3 meters) were found on Greek islands (Crete, Cyclades, Dodecanese). Cf. Symeonides, N. K.; et al. (2001). 'New data on Palaeoloxodon chaniensis (Vamos cave, Chania, Crete)'. In Cavarretta, Giuseppe (ed.), The World of Elephants - International Congress, Rome 2001, Rome 2001, 510-513; Theodorou, G., The dwarf elephants of the Charkadio cave on the island of Tilos (Dodekanese, Greece). PhD Thesis Athens University, 1983. Also, the mammoth with the longest tusks in the world is found outside the northern Greek city of Ptolemais. They are 3,5 meters long, weighing 6 tons and they were discovered by Prof. Evagelia Tsoukala from the Aristotelian University of Thessaloniki.

Chapter 1
Humanoid Monsters

The first thing that springs to mind when one thinks of ancient Greek monsters is some gruesome hybrid that verges between human and animal form or some hideous creature that resembles none of the common forms of life, as the Greeks knew them. However, monsters may look almost like us, only slightly different. Sometimes they differ in size, sometimes they differ in habits and sometimes they differ due to their ancestry or habitat. Humanoid monsters may be distinguished by some singular physical characteristic that constitutes monstrosity. There are many humanoid creatures in Greek myth and they deserve a special place in the gallery of the unusual.

Arimaspians (Ἀριμασποί)

Aristeas of Proconessus was a poet who supposedly lived around the 7th c. BC.[18] He is mentioned by Herodotus in book 4 of his *Histories*. Aristeas is responsible for the account of some fabulous creatures, such as the tribe of Arimaspians (Ἀριμασποί), as well as the Griffins, in a lost epic called *Arimaspea*. The Arismaspians, a race which lived in the north, were one-eyed, and neighbours to the land of the mythical Grypes (the Griffins):

> *This Aristeas, possessed by Phoibos, visited the Issedones; beyond these (he said) live the one-eyed Arimaspoi, beyond whom are the Grypes that guard gold, and beyond these again the Hyperboreoi, whose territory reaches the sea. Except for the Hyperboreoi, all these nations (and first the Arimaspoi) are always at war with their neighbours.*[19]

According to Herodotus, the name derives from the Scythian tongue, in which 'arima' means *one* and 'spou' is the eye.[20] However, Hesiod is very cautious when he refers to one-eyed human tribes. 'I do not believe this, that there are one-eyed men who have a nature otherwise the same as other men. The most outlying lands,

---

[18] For the benefit of the non specialist readers I have generally used the more popular versions of Greek names (i.e. Achilles instead of Achilleus, or Dionysus instead of Dionysos. However, in quotations I preserved the names as written in the source from which I drew the quotation.
[19] Herodotus, 4. 13. 1.
[20] Herodotus, 4. 27.

though, as they enclose and wholly surround the rest of the world, are likely to have those things which we think the finest and the rarest'.[21]

The land of the Arimaspoi and the Grypes is also mentioned by the 5th c. BC playwright Aeschylus (Aesch. *Prometheus Bound*).[22] In the play about the punishment of Prometheus, Io appears, the priestess of Hera at a temple in Argos, whom Zeus fell in love with. [23] At some point, she reaches mount Caucasus, where the Titan Prometheus is bound by Hephaestus, by order of Zeus, because he has stolen fire from heaven and given it to mortals. Prometheus advised her to avoid the land of the Arimaspians and the Griffins and head south. In this passage, more monstrous creatures are mentioned, such as the Gorgons and the three old women, the daughters of Phorcys:

> [790] When you have crossed the stream that bounds the two continents, toward the flaming east, where the sun walks,...... crossing the surging sea until you reach the Gorgonean plains of Cisthene, where the daughters of Phorcys dwell, ancient maids, [795] three in number, shaped like swans, possessing one eye amongst them and a single tooth; neither does the sun with his beams look down upon them, nor ever the nightly moon. And near them are their three winged sisters, the snake-haired Gorgons, loathed by mankind, [800] whom no one of mortal kind shall look upon and still draw breath. Such is the peril that I bid you to guard against. But now listen to another and a fearsome spectacle. Beware of the sharp-beaked hounds of Zeus that do not bark, the gryphons, [805] and the one-eyed Arimaspian folk, mounted on horses, who dwell about the flood of Pluto's stream that flows with gold. Do not approach them. Then you shall come to a far-off country of a dark race that dwells by the waters of the sun, where the river Aethiop is. [810] Follow along its banks until you reach the cataract, where, from the Bybline mountains, Nile sends forth his hallowed and sweet stream. He will conduct you on your way to the three-angled land of Nilotis, where, at last, it is ordained for you, [815] O Io, and for your children to found your far-off colony.[24]

---

[21] Herodotus, 3.116 (transl. by A. D. Godley).
[22] Myres (1946) 2-4; Cheremisin & Zaporozhchenko (1999) 228-231.
[23] Apollod. 2.1.3: Zeus seduced her while she held the priesthood of Hera, but being detected by Hera he by a touch turned Io into a white cow and swore that he had not known her; wherefore Hesiod remarks that lover's oaths do not draw down the anger of the gods. But Hera requested the cow from Zeus for herself and set Argus the All-seeing to guard it (transl. by Sir James George Frazer).
[24] Aeschylus, Prometheus 790-815 Transl. by H.W. Smyth).

Herodotus' cautionary attitude regarding these strange people was not shared by later writers.[25] Diodorus Siculus reported that Alexander the Great had met with them, although he says nothing about their singular characteristic. He calls them Benefactors, because they had helped Cyrus in times of dire straits. According to this account, the army of Cyrus ran out of food during a long campaign into the desert. Famished and desperate, the soldiers of Cyrus were constrained to eat each other. The Arimaspians showed up bringing thirty thousand wagons laid with provisions. In gratitude Cyrus granted them tax-exemption and named them Benefactors.[26] Strabo mentions them in his *Geography*, as people 'who lived across the Caspian'.[27] T. Maccius Plautus (c. 254–184 BC) quotes Pliny the Elder, who describes the similarity between the Cyclops and the Arimaspians, 'a nation of Sarmatia, as having but one eye'.[28]

Blemmyae (Βλέμμυαι)

The remote lands of Africa were always prosperous grounds for nurturing stranger kinds of people. Herodotus in the 5th c. B.C. is the first who described most of them for the first time. In his *Histories* he describes the Blemmyae (Βλέμμυαι, perhaps from βλέμμα, gaze and μέσον, middle: the ones who see from the middle). In his 4th book of his amazing *Histories* he reports a strange savage tribe of people whose faces are set on their chest.

> *For the eastern region of Libya [i.e. North Africa], which the nomads inhabit, is low-lying and sandy as far as the Triton river; but the land west of this, where the farmers live, is exceedingly mountainous and wooded and full of wild beasts. In that country are the huge snakes and the lions, and the elephants and bears and asps, the horned asses, the Dog-Headed (Kynokephaloi) and the Headless (Akephaloi) men that have their eyes in their chests, as the Libyans say, and the wild men and women, besides many other creatures not fabulous.*[29]

Recent scholarship has often wondered whether such descriptions simply allude to a tribe of warriors, who stealthily preyed upon the animals they were hunting, ducked so low, that their head seemed to disappear in their chest. Rather than searching for futile rational explanations as this, it is more fruitful to observe

---

[25] Modern scholarship still debates about the historicity of these peoples. Rival theories in antiquity variously locating Hyperboreans and Arimaspi are explored by Casson, (February - March 1920)1–3; Bolton (1962) places them on the upper Irtysh and on the slopes of the Altai.
[26] Diodorus, 17.81; Cf. Curtius 7.33 Arrian 3.27.4-5.
[27] Strabo, Geography 11. 6.
[28] T. Maccius Plautus, Curculio, or the Forgery, act. 3, scene 1.
[29] Herodotus, Histories 4. 191. 3 (transl. Godley).

the evolution of such stories in works of later writers, such as Pliny the Elder (1st c. A.D.) who draws apparently not from Herodotus, but from another historian whose work is lost, Ctesias:

> Ctesias [Greek historian C4th B.C.] writes that . . . westward from these [the Troglodytoi of the Red Sea coast of Africa] there are some people without necks, having eyes on their shoulders.[30]

Alexander encounters the headless men (gens sans teste), miniature from Historia de proelis in French (cf. Roman d'Alexandre en prose), in the Talbot Shrewsbury Book (BL Royal MS 15 E vi), f. 21v. Held and digitised by the British Library

---

[30] Pliny the Elder, *Natural History*, 7. 23 (transl. Rackham).

Later scholars relied totally upon his accounts. Strabo quoted Herodotus, but he described the Blemmyae simply as nomads, not many in number and certainly not great fighters.31 For Pliny, the creatures have more weird a look, since they have no face at all, just eyes on their shoulders. In the 7th c. A. D., St. Isidore from Seville, known in Latin sources as Isidorus Hispalensis (c. 560- April 636 A.D.) composed an etymological dictionary, better, a kind of Encyclopedia of universal knowledge, entitled *Etymologiae*, in which he wrote: 'legend has it, that the Blemmyae of Libya are born without heads, with eyes and a mouth on their chest or without a neck, so that their eyes are set upon their shoulders'.[32]

Cyclopes (Κύκλωπες)

A single eye on a massive forehead, a gigantic body of primitive wildness, voracious appetite for milk, wine and human flesh... enter Cyclops ... in the cave where Odysseus and his trembling companions cower in fear at this sight. Homer immortalized Polyphemus by recording his encounter with Odysseus, but others, too, are named by Hesiod in his *Theogony*: Brontes, Steropes and Arges were sons of the prime gods Sky and Earth. They were brothers of the Titans, most of them craftsmen; only the Cyclopes were mortal. In the *Theogony* of Hesiod, one of our most extant version of this story, Earth gives birth to the Giants after the Titans and before their monstrous brothers, the hundred-handed Hecatoncheires.

> *First Sky ruled over the entire world. He married Earth and Produced Briareus, Gyes, and Cottus, the so-called Hundred-Handed, who possessed a hundred hands and fifty heads and were unsurpassed in size and strength.*[33]
> *And again, she bare the Cyclopes, overbearing in spirit, Brontes and Steropes and stubborn-headed Arges, who gave Zeus the thunder and made the thunderbolt: in all else they were like the gods, but one eye only was set in the midst of their foreheads. And they were surnamed Cyclopes (Orb-eyed) because one orbed eye was set in their foreheads. Strength and craft were in their works.*[34]

Hesiod knows only three of them and their names definitely associate them with their celestial father, Uranus. Brontes *the Thunderer,* Steropes *the Lightner* and Arges *the Vivid,* gain their prominent place in the world of Greek myths during the war that Zeus waged against Cronus, his own father, who had developed a voracious

---

[31] Strabo, book 17, 1.2 and 1.53.
[32] For the survival of Blemmyae in Medieval literature see Katie Walter(2013) 16 ff.
[33] Apollodorus, Library, 1. 1-2 (transl. Simpson).
[34] Hesiod, Theogony, 139-146 (transl. Evelyn-White).

appetite for his very own children. Cronus, spurred on by his own mother, attacked his father Uranus in his sleep, castrated him and overthrew him from his reign. In fear of losing his newly acquired throne to one of his children, he ordered his wife Rhea to bring them to him, so that he would eat them. Equally concerned of the strength of the Cyclopes and the Hundred-handers, he imprisoned them in the depths of Tartarus[35] Rhea saved Zeus by offering Cronus a stone wrapped up in baby-clothes. Then she took the infant god to a cave in Crete, where he grew hidden from the eyes of his father and nurtured by a goat named Amaltheia. When he reached maturity, he attacked Cronus and somehow – mythology does not care about such functional details – he forced Cronus to disgorge his brothers and sisters who had been swallowed before him.[36] Hestia, Demeter, Hera, Hades and Poseidon were rescued by Zeus and stood on the side of their brother. Some of the older gods, the Titans, sided with Cronus. In order to have powerful allies, Zeus freed the Cyclopes and the Hecatoncheires, the Hundred-handers, from Tartarus after killing Campe, the monster that was set to guard them.[37]

Once freed, the Cyclopes stood on Zeus' side. Their role was vital for the victory of Zeus since they were skilled craftsmen and blacksmiths and they forged the most formidable of weapons for their rescuer, the thunderbolt. The trident of Poseidon and a magical cap that makes its bearer invisible – a gift for Hades – are their works, too. With such an arsenal at his disposal Zeus overcame the Titans and it was their time to be thrown into Tartarus. The Cyclopes were rewarded with the great honour of continuing to manufacture the thunderbolts of Zeus. Unfortunately, one of them was used to kill the son of Apollo, Asclepius. Angered with the Cyclopes, Apollo killed all three of them.

A different version about the origin of the Cyclopes is found in the *Odyssey* of Homer. At least one of them, perhaps the most notorious Cyclops in literature, is a child of Poseidon and the nymph Thoosa.[38]

In the *Odyssey*, Cyclopes stand for the opposite of civilization and order to be found in the advanced culture of the Greek city-state. Primitive and wild, the Cyclopes live off animal husbandry, they do not plough the earth or harvest crops,

---

[35] Tartarus was one of the primal entities of the Universe, along with Earth and Eros. It was also the name of a dark and terrible region so deep below the earth that an iron anvil dropped from the surface of the ground would need nine days to reach this place. Cf. Homer, Iliad, 8.10-17, 478-81; Hesiod, Theogony 119, 713-35, 820-22; Apollodorus 1.1.4-5, 1.6.3, 2.1.2, 3.10.4; Virgil, Aeneid 6.548-627.
[36] Hesiod, Theogony,453-506.
[37] Virgil, Aeneid 7.803-17, 11.432-3, 498-868.
[38] Cf. Aguirre Castro (1999) 14-22.

like humans, they don't have laws to respect and they have no sense of community, as Odysseus vividly describes:

> 'From there, grieving still at heart, we sailed on further   105
> along, and reached the country of the lawless outrageous
> Cyclopes who, putting all their trust in the immortal
> gods, neither plow with their hands nor plant anything,
> but all grows for them without seed planting, without cultivation,
> wheat and barley and also the grapevines, which yield for them   110
> wine of strength, and it is Zeus' rain that waters it for them.
> These people have no institutions, no meetings for counsels;
> rather they make their habitations in caverns hollowed
> among the peaks of the high mountains, and each one is the law
> for his own wives and children, and cares nothing about
> the others.[39]   115

Odysseus arrived at the island of the Cyclopes.[40] He and some of his companions found his cave, full of milk, cheese and everything one might expect to find in a shepherd's den. The men urge Odysseus to grab whatever supplies they can and leave quickly, but Odysseus, curious and perhaps driven by a sense of honesty, convinces them to stay and find out what sort of man lives in a place like this and see whether he can get what he wants in the reciprocal manner of gifts' exchange. When the monstrous figure of Polyphemus enters the cave, fear seizes them all. They hide at first, but they are soon discovered. Odysseus' courteous efforts to awake in him respect for the sacred laws of hospitality fail pitifully. The humans will soon find out not only that they won't be offered the customary dinner of hospitality, but they will serve as dinner themselves.

> 'So I spoke, but he in pitiless spirit answered
> nothing, but sprang up and reached for my companions,
> caught up two together and slapped them, like killing puppies,
> against the ground and the brains ran all over the floor, soaking   290
> the ground. Then he cut them up limb by limb and got supper ready,

---

[39] Homer, Odyssey, 9. 105-115 (transl. Lattimore).
[40] The location of this island was a mystery to ancient writers. Thucydides (6.2) located it near the coast of Sicily, close to mount Aetna. Virgil (Aeneid 8. 416ff) describes the forge of Hephaestus/Vulcan, where the Cyclopes labor as smiths, on a small island called Vulcania, in the north of Sicily. However, in his Georgics (4.170-73) and in the Aeneid (3.569-71) he locates them at mount Aetna in Sicily. Cf. Simpson (1976) 23, n. 3.

*and like a lion reared in the hills, without leaving anything,
ate them, entrails, flesh and marrowy bones alike. We
cried out aloud and held our hands up to Zeus, seeing
the cruelty of what he did, but our hearts were helpless.   295
But when the Cyclops had filled his enormous stomach, feeding
on human flesh and drinking down milk unmixed with water,
he lay down to sleep in the cave sprawled out through his sheep.*[41]

Odysseus and his crew are blinding Polyphemus. Detail of a Proto-Attic amphora, circa 650 BC. Eleusis, Archaeological Museum, Inv. 2630.

---

[41] Homer, Odyssey, 9. 287-297 (transl. Lattimore).

Six of Odysseus' men had the same fate, before Odysseus tricked him with wine unmixed with water. The repercussions of drinking undiluted wine are more catastrophic for Polyphemus than drinking undiluted milk – although, perhaps equally uncivilized. The ogre passed out drunk and Odysseus blinded him with a wooden stake hardened in fire. This was necessary so that Polyphemus would remove the huge boulder with which he had blocked the cave's entrance. Like a good shepherd, the monster had to let his flock out to pasture in the morning. Odysseus and his men clung under the bellies of the sheep and thus escaped from the cave. However, Odysseus did not escape the wrath of Poseidon who tormented Odysseus for many years at sea, before he finally managed to return back to Ithaca.

Cynocephaloi and Akephaloi (Κυνοκέφαλοι & Ακέφαλοι)

Africa breeds many tribes of monstrous humanoid tribes. Cynocephaloi, the Dog-headed people[42] (Κυνοκέφαλοι) and Acephaloi, the Headless (Ακέφαλοι), dwell the lands of Lydia, according to Herodotus, or the Indian mountains, according to Ctesias. Herodotus reports that the Cynocephaloi lived in the eastern region of Libya, as well as the Headless Men:

> *For the eastern region of Libya, which the Nomads inhabit, is low-lying and sandy as far as the Triton river; but the land west of this, where the farmers live, is exceedingly mountainous and wooded and full of wild beasts. In that country are the huge snakes and the lions, and the elephants and bears and asps, the horned asses, the Kunokephaloi (Cynocephali) (Dog-Headed) and the Headless Men that have their eyes in their chests, as the Libyans say, and the wild men and women, besides many other creatures not fabulous.*[43]

---

[42] Modern theories associate the Dog-headed people with baboons, which were mistaken for men by travellers, such as Herodotus. Aelian's description of the eating habits and techniques of these people, certainly enhances this interpretation: If a Kynokephalos finds some edible object with a shell on it (like almonds, acorns, nuts) it strips the shell off and cleans it out, after first breaking it most intelligently, and it knows that the contents are good to eat but that the outside is to be thrown away. And it will drink wine, and if boiled or cooked meat is served to it, it will eat its fill; and it likes well-seasoned food, but it dislikes food boiled without any care. If it wears clothes, it is careful of them; and it does everything else that I have described. If you put it while still tiny on a woman's breast, it will suck the milk like a baby. (Aelian, On Animals, 10. 30). Transl. Scholfield.
[43] Herodotus, Histories 4. 191. 3 (transl. Godley).

It is not clear whether they should be identified with the Hemicynes, the Half-Dog men, described by Hesiod in the fragments of his *Catalogues of Women*.[44]

The longest extant description of these people is still the account of Ctesias (4th c. BC) in his lost *Indica*, which has survived in the work of later writers and was summarized by the 9th c. AD scholar Photius in his *Myriobiblon* (Μυριόβιβλον ἢ Βιβλιοθήκη).

> On these [the Indian] mountains there live men with the head of a dog, whose clothing is the skin of wild beasts. They speak no language, but bark like dogs, and in this manner make themselves understood by each other. Their teeth are larger than those of dogs, their nails like those of these animals, but longer and rounder. They inhabit the mountains as far as the river Indos. Their complexion is swarthy. They are extremely just, like the rest of the Indians with whom they associate. They understand the Indian language but are unable to converse, only barking or making signs with their hands and fingers by way of reply, like the deaf and dumb. They are called by the Indians Kalystrii, in Greek Kynocephaloi (Cynocephali) (Dog-Headed). They live on raw meat and number about 120,000 ... The Cynocephaloi living on the mountains do not practise any trade but live on hunting. When they have killed an animal they roast it in the sun. They also rear numbers of sheep, goats, and asses, drinking the milk of the sheep and whey made from it. They eat the fruit of the Siptakhora, whence amber is procured, since it is sweet. They also dry it and keep it in baskets, as the Greeks keep their dried grapes. They make rafts which they load with this fruit together with well-cleaned purple flowers and 260 talents of amber, with the same quantity of the purple dye, and 1000 additional talents of amber, which they send annually to the king of India. They exchange the rest for bread, flour, and cotton stuffs with the Indians, from whom they also buy swords for hunting wild beasts, bows, and arrows, being very skilful in drawing the bow and hurling the spear. They cannot be defeated in war, since they inhabit lofty and inaccessible mountains. Every five years the king sends them a present of 300,000 bows, as many spears, 120,000 shields, and 50,000 swords. They do not live in houses, but in caves. They set out for the chase with bows and spears, and as they are very swift of foot, they pursue and soon overtake their

---

[44] [The Boreades pursued the Harpyiai (Harpies)] to the lands of the Massagetai and of the proud Hemikunes (Hemicynes) (Half-dog men), of the Katoudaioi (Catoudaei) (Underground-folk) ... Huge Gaia (Earth) bare these to Epaphos ... Aithiopes (Ethiopians) and Libys [i.e. Gaia was the mother by Epaphos of all the African tribes]: Hesiod, Catalogues of Women, fragment 40A (from the Oxyrhynchus Papyri 1358). Cf. Hesiod, Catalogues of Women, fragment 44, which mentions also the Macrocephaloi (Long-Headed Men) and the Pygmaioi (Pygmies).

quarry. The women have a bath once a month the men do not have a bath at all, but only wash their hands. They anoint themselves three times a month with oil made from milk and wipe themselves with skins. The clothes of men and women alike are not skins with the hair on, but skins tanned and very fine. The richest wear linen clothes, but they are few in number. They have no beds, but sleep on leaves or grass. He who possesses the greatest number of sheep is considered the richest, and so in regard to their other possessions. All, both men and women, have tails above their hips, like dogs, but longer and more hairy. They are just, and live longer than any other men, 170, sometimes 200 years.[45]

Cynocephali illustrated in the Kievan psalter, 1397

---

[45] Ctesias, Indica Fragment (summary from Photius, Myriobiblon) (transl. Freese).

In the second century AD, *Aelian* placed the Cynocephaloi in India as well and he explained that they owe their name to their physical appearance and nature. He also accepted that apart from their dog-head, they resemble humans. They wear animal skins and they are harmless. According to Aelian, they also lack speech and they can only howl like dogs, although they can comprehend the Indian language. Obviously influenced by Herodotus, Aelian reports that 'wild animals are their food, and they catch them with the utmost ease, for they are exceedingly swift of foot; and when they have caught them they kill and cook them, not over a fire but by exposing them to the sun's heat after they have shredded them into pieces. They also keep goats and sheep, and while their food is the flesh of wild beasts, their drink is the milk of the animals they keep. I have mentioned them along with brute beasts, as is logical, for their speech is inarticulate, unintelligible and not that of man'.[46]

Aelian distinguishes the Dog-Headed men from the Dog-Faced Men (Cynoprosopoi). They can be found after a seven-day journey beyond the Egyptian oasis, along the road that leads to Ethiopia. They are black in appearance, do not talk but utter a shrill squeal and they have a long beard on their chin, which Aelian compares to the beard of Drakones (dragons). Their nails are very sharp and strong and they are hard to capture, for they are very fast and very familiar with their surroundings.[47]

The Dog-Headed Men are mentioned also by Pliny the Elder (1st c. AD), who locates them in Africa too, at the Aethiopian kingdom of Meroe along with the Medimni, the strange Alabi, who live on the milk of the Cynocephali and the Syrbotae 'who are said to be 12 feet high'.[48] With regard to their location, Pliny also quotes Megasthenes, a Greek historian of the 4th c. BC, who placed the Cynocephaloi in the Indian mountains. Their characteristics and number are just like those described by Herodotus, with the interesting addition that they can use their nails as weapons.[49]

Giants (Γίγαντες)

Unless some of the immortal gods of the skies have come,
then gods devise something else for us,
for so far they appear in front of us as they are, without changing their form,
every time we offer them brilliant sacred sacrifices.

---

[46] Aelian, On Animals, 4.46.
[47] Aelian, On Animals, 0.25.
[48] Pliny the Elder, Natural History, 6. 194.
[49] Pliny the Elder, Natural History, 7. 23.

And they dine with us, sitting at our tables.
And if one of us roams the roads and happens to cross their path,
they do not hide from him; for we are related to them,
as the Cyclopes and the wild Giants are related.[50]

This is the oldest literary reference to the race of Giants (Γίγαντες, singular: Γίγας). These words are uttered by king Alcinous of the Phaecians when he speaks of his people's origins. He is looking at Odysseus, stranded on his island, and he is wondering whether he is one of the gods. For him, it would be strange to consider that Odysseus might be one of the gods, since the gods do not take human form in order to appear in front of the Phaeacians.[51] From the text it is not very clear whether Alcinous implies that the gods and the Phaeacians are related just like the Cyclopes and the Giants are related to each other, or whether gods, Phaeacians and Cyclopes are all related. No matter what the real meaning is, it is used to project the exceptional status of Alcinous' people and to impress Odysseus. It also correlates beyond doubt two of the most ancient monstrous races of mythology: the Giants and the Cyclopes.

The name Γίγαντες (Giants) most probably relates them to their mother, Gaea (Γαία), the Earth – γηγενής means *born of the earth*, thus γηγενής-γίγας relates them to Earth.[52] One of our earlier sources, Hesiod, says that they were born from drops of blood that fell on the Earth after the mutilation of Uranus (the Sky) by his son Cronus.[53] The Erinyes, the fierce goddesses of fury and vengeance and the Melian Nymphs, were born in the same way. According to Nonnus (5th c. A.D.) they were one hundred of them – at least this is what we infer from the phrase ' the coiling

---

[50] Homer, Odyssey, 7. 200-205 (transl. Syropoulos).

[51] It must be the only case that humans see – or so they claim – the real form of divinity. For the truth is that no man knows what God looks like. God may take any form he or she desires. Zeus kidnapped Europa in the form of a bull and he mated with Leda in the form of a swan. Even a jail did not deter him from uniting with Andromeda, the mother of Perseus, in the form of rain. And when gods want to communicate with humans, they need to take up a form that humans can relate to. It is in human form that he had a passionate relationship with the young princess of Thebes, Semele. And when she, after a device of jealous Hera, demanded from Zeus to appear in front of her in his real form, she was consumed by living fire and thunders – this is what god really looks like. Apollodorus, iii. 4. § 3; Ovid, Metamorphoses iii. 260ff; Hyginus. Fabulae 179.

[52] Homer, Odyssey 7. 59. Cf. Gantz (1996) 16 and Hard (2004) 86

[53] Hesiod, Theogony, 178-86.

sons of Earth with two hundred hands'.[54] Hesiod in his *Theogony* gives us the most detailed account of their birth.[55] He writes:

> *As each of his children was born, Uranus hid them all in the depths of Ge [i.e. the Earth] and did not allow them to emerge into the light. And he delighted in his wickedness. But huge Earth in her distress groaned within and fashioned a great sickle and confided in her dear children. Sorrowing in her heart she urged them as follows: 'My children, born of a presumptuous father, if you are willing to obey, we shall punish his evil insolence. For he was the first to devise shameful actions.'*
>
> *Thus she spoke. Fear seized them all and not one answered. But great and wily Cronus took courage and spoke to his dear mother: 'I shall undertake and accomplish the deed, since I do not care about our abominable father. For he was the first to devise shameful actions.'*
>
> *Thus he spoke. And huge Earth rejoiced greatly in her heart. She hid him in an ambush and placed in his hands the sickle with jagged teeth and revealed the whole plot to him. Great Uranus came leading on night, and, desirous of love, lay on Ge, spreading himself over her completely. And his son from his ambush reached out with his left hand and in his right he seized hold of the huge sickle with jagged teeth and swiftly cut off the genitals of his own dear father and threw them so that they fell behind him. And they did not fall from his hand in vain. Earth received all the bloody drops that fell and in the course of the seasons bore the strong Erinyes and might giants (shining in their armor and carrying longs spears in their hands) and nymphs of ash trees (called Meliae on the wide earth).*[56]

It is evident in this version that the Giants were nothing but huge human-like beings, with long spears and clad in shiny armour; at least in the *Theogony* of Hesiod.[57] This is how they appear in most of the vase paintings of the archaic and classical period. As we move on towards the Hellenistic period, though, things change. First of all, there is the war between the Giants and the gods of Olympus. During the Hellenistic and Roman era the clash between the two races became synonymous to the struggle of civilized peoples against barbarians and this symbolism is echoed in the poetry and art of those times.

---

[54] Nonnus, Dionysiaca, 25. 85.
[55] Hesiod, Theogony, 178-87.
[56] Hesiod, Theogony 256f (transl. Morford & Lenardon).
[57] Cf. Ovid, Amores, 2. 1. 11.

HUMANOID MONSTERS 23

Poseidon (left) holding a trident, with the island Nisyros on his shoulder, battling a Giant (probably Polybotes), red-figure cup c. 500–450 BC (Cabinet des Medailles 573)

The famous battle of the Giants against the gods, known as *Gigantomachy*, is mentioned neither by Homer nor Hesiod in the 8th c. B.C. The most extant bibliographical account is found in Apollodorus in the 2nd c. A.D. and this is most probably based on an Alexandrian story of the 3rd c. B.C. However, vase painters were fascinated with the theme of the battle of the Giants as early as the archaic period and sculptors of the 5th c. B.C. used the theme to promote the idea of the first honorable defensive war; this is why it was depicted on the Acropolis of Athens, after the Persian wars. The Persians were obviously the unjust invaders of the free land of Greece. The analogy with the battle of the Giants against Zeus and his brothers and sisters served the propagandistic policy of Athens, at the time when it had already started oppressing the rest of the Greek city-states and it needed to advertise not only its superior status, through the magnificent architecture of the Parthenon, but also its role as a defender of justice and a champion of the Greek city states against the Persians.

Giants change. Because of their barbarous connotations, they become more monstrous. Size is not enough. Now they gain tremendous strength, fierce characteristics in faces covered by long beards and long hair. Their feet are now scaly or they are replaced by snake bodies. And they turned against the Olympian gods.

The cause of this great war, the second biggest the universe had witnessed until then – the first one, of course, being the Titanomachy – was Earth. It was Earth who was angered with Zeus, because he had exterminated the Titans, her children. [58]To punish him, she bore the giants. In the ensuing battle all gods, with the exception of Demeter, took part. According to some of our older myths, the battlefield was on earth, at a place called Phlegrae, which means 'blazing fields', or a place in Macedonia, called Pallene.[59] It seems that this time Earth took the part of the Giants openly – also the hundred-handed Hecatoncheires. It was not only that Zeus had subdued the Titans and the terrible Typhoeus, but the fact that the new gods had taken the side of Uranus, the Sky, whom Earth was always against.[60] It seems that the battle was so ambiguous, that the new gods did not consider it beneath them to ask for the help of people born from mortal mothers, such as Dionysus and Hercules.[61]

The description of the battle scenes is very vivid and it varies from writer to writer; the most detailed one is probably to be found in Apollodorus' *Library* 1.1.1-1.6.3). According to him, the battle was terrible. Some of the gods and demi-gods stood out, like Zeus, Athena and Hercules. Amongst the Giants, Porphyrion and Alcyoneus were the most formidable ones. Hercules shot an arrow at Alcyoneus, but each time the Giant fell on Earth (i.e. his mother) his strength was revived. It was Athena who advised Hercules to drag Alcyoneus beyond his native ground of Pallene, and so he died. As for Porphyrion, love, or rather lust, was his doom. Zeus

---

[58] The names of the Titans are recorded by Apollodorus :' Ocean, Coeus, Hyperion, Crius, Iapetus and Cronus, the youngest of all. He [i.e. the Sky] also had daughters called Titanides: Tethys, Rhea, Themis, Mnemosyne, Phoebe, Dione and Thia' (Library, 1. 3).

[59] Apollonius, 1. 6. 1 Alternative locations include Campania of Italy, close to the volcano Vesuvius, or a place in Arcadia, Greece, called Bathos.

[60] Apollonius, 1. 6. 1.

[61] Technically, Dionysus is born both of a mortal womb and Zeus himself. Before his mother Semele was burned by Zeus, he had the time to take her unborn child and sew it in his thigh. Thus, Dionysus is born not of a mortal womb but of a god, therefore he is immortal.

inflicted upon him lust for Hera, and when the Giant attacked her, Zeus struck him with a thunderbolt and Hercules finished him off with one of his arrows.

The Giant Eurytus was killed by Dionysus by a thyrsus (a kind of reed with a pointed cone on top). Apollo killed Ephialtes with his bow. Hecate, goddess of the underworld and the moon, burned Mimas with her torches and Hephaestus hurled hot-metal on Mimas. The Giant Enceladus was a fire-breathing monster. Athena threw a whole island on top of the Giant Enceladus. It was the island of Sicily and since then, Enceladus' blazing breath erupts through the top of mount Aetna. Pallas was another monstrous Giant, whom Athena killed and used his skin as a shield. Another island was used as a weapon by the gods. This time it was Poseidon's turn to throw a piece of the island of Cos on top of the Giant Polybotes; this piece is now the island of Nisyros. Hermes, wearing the cap of invisibility that belonged to Hades, killed Hippolytus. Gration was killed by Artemis and even the ancient three Fates, Clotho, Lachesis and Atropos, killed Agrius and Thoas with cudgels of bronze.[62]

Writers in later scholarship tried to rationalize the myth, considering the Giants nothing more than barbaric tribes of fierce warriors. Diodorus Siculus (1st c. BC) recounts the labours of Hercules and describes the Giants as impressive warriors living at Cyme:

> *Hercules, now, set off from the Tiber, passed from the shore of what today is called Italy and reached the plain of Cyme, where, according to legend, there were men who were distinguished for their physical strength and were famous for their illegality, called giants. Also, the valley was called Phlegraia, from the hill which in the old days, threw up huge fires more or less like Aetna in Sicily. Today the hill is called Vesuvius and has many scars from the fire which it emitted since the ancient times. The Giants, then, as soon as they had learned about the appearance of Hercules, gathered together and set in line to face him. The battle that followed was wonderful for the strength and courage of the giants and they say that Hercules allied with the gods to prevail and so, after killing most, tamed the area. According to myth, the giants were native in this area because of their excessive size; such are the myths told by some about the giants killed in Phlegra and they were followed by the writer Timaeos.*[63]

The monstrosity of Giants is evident not only in their appearance but also in their character. Diodorus Siculus (1st c. A.D.) describes the Giants as being contemporary to the mythical Telchines who dwelled within the island of Rhodes

---

[62] Cf. March, Giants (2014) 204.
[63] Diodorus, Library, 4.21.5 (transl. Syropoulos).

in the a-temporal mythical past. He reports that there were three of them and describes their insolent character. They denied even the sacred value of hospitality to Aphrodite, when she attempted to debark on the coast of Rhodes while travelling from the island of Cythera to Cyprus:

5 *And at this period in the eastern parts of the island there sprung up the Giants, as they were called; and at the time when Zeus is said to have subdued the Titans, he became enamoured of one of the nymphs, Himalia by name, and begat by her three sons, Spartaeus, Cronius, and Cytus.* 6 And while these were still young men, Aphroditê, they say, as she was journeying from Cytherae to Cyprus and dropped anchor near Rhodes, was prevented from stopping there by the sons of Poseidon, who were arrogant and insolent men; whereupon the goddess, in her wrath, brought madness *upon them, and they lay with their mother against her will and committed many acts of violence upon the natives.* 7 But when Poseidon learned of what had happened he buried his sons beneath the earth, because of their shameful deed, and men called them the ‹Eastern Demons›; and Halia cast herself into the sea, *and she was afterwards given the name of Leucothea and attained to immortal honour in the eyes of the natives.*[64]

Nearly every known culture preserves myths about giants who fought with the first mortals. In the Koran, they are men of the Aant and Hount nations, tall and powerful, able to uproot a whole tree with bare hands. They became disobedient and turned against God and the Prophet and thus they were destroyed. North American Indians relate stories about giants. The people of the tribe of Iroquis tell stories about their prime god, Hi'nuun, god of thunders, who destroyed the race of stone-giants with the help of his brother, the Western Wind.[65] Giants who uproot trees with their hands are found in the myths of the Aztecs, when the first world is ruled by the Black Tezkatlipoka. Also the Mayas talk about Caprakan, the god of earthquakes and mountains, who is a son of giants. The ancient Mexicans remember the giants named Quinametzim, who dwelt the earth in a very distant past and fought against humans. In Australia, the myths of Kakadu tribe mention no gods, only one giant, Vuraka. He was the creator of the mountains Roe and Bintvel, which he created after having walked along the western coast and reached the area called Alukalandi. The Great Mother, Iberomera, who already carried lots of children in her womb, asked him to walk with her, but he was tired. So, she carried on alone and went to various lands where she left her children and many different tongues behind. Giants are prominent also in Scandinavian mythology. When the universe consisted only of chaos and darkness, a great frozen chasm divided the land of ice and cold in the north from the land of light and fire in the south. The Giant of Fire caused sparks with his sword and these sparks reached the

---

[64] Diodorus, Library, 5 55.5 (transl. Oldfather, p249a).
[65] Spense (1914) 217.

chasm and created vapours. The vapours froze and fell like snow over the chasm and from this snow the forefather of the Ice Giants, Imir, was born, along with a gigantic cow. Imir suckled the cow, but as he was hungry, he started licking the ice until he uncovered the god Buri. He was the father of Bor, who married a giant woman and had three sons, Odin, Vili and Ve. They are the first of the Aisir tribe, the powers of Good and principal deities of the northerners who constantly fought the Giants. Indian tradition includes mythical beings called giants and Japanese myths call them Wild Kami. In the *Old Testament*, Moses sends spies to report on the people of Canaan. The spies found giants from the tribe of Nephileem: *...those who we saw there, are extremely tall, and we saw the giants there, the sons of Anak from the race of the giants; compared to them we seemed like grasshoppers and as such they regarded us, too.*[66]

Phorcids (Graeae, Gorgons & Sirens) – Φόρκυς (Γραίαι, Γοργόνες, Σειρήνες)

Phorcys (Φόρκυς) is a god of the sea, a child of the ancient Pontos (the Sea) and Gaia (the Earth).[67] His name might be associated to φώκιες, seals. In resemblance to other royal couples (Zeus and Hera, Poseidon and Amphitrite) Phorcys is married to a sea-goddess who was his sister, by the name of Keto (Κητώ, meaning 'whale' or 'sea monster'. On a mosaic from Antioch dated around the 4th c. AD (now in Antakya Museum) he is depicted as a grey-haired man with the tail of a fish. Many popular monstrous offsprings are fathered by him. His sister/wife bore him the Graeae and the Gorgons,[68] the dragon of Hesperia,[69] and the Hesperides, the keepers of the golden apples that Hercules had to find for Eurystheus.[70] By Hecate

---

[66] Old Testament, Numbers 13, 33. In the 5th and last book of the Old Testament (called Δευτερονόμιον) there is a description of Vasan as 'Giant land' (3.13). Giants lived in this mountainous area before the cataclysm and they survived until the days of Abraham. When Hodollogomor and his allies went to fight with the army of Sodom and Gomorra, they destroyed the giants of the cities Astaroth and Karnain at Vasan (Genesis, 14,5). Perhaps one of the last giants was Goliath, an ally of the Philistines who was killed by David (Ά Βασιλειών 17, 4).
[67] Hesiod, Theogony 237; Apollodorus, Library 1. 2. 6, 10. In Homer he is described as 'the old man of the sea', to whom a harbour of Ithaca was dedicated. Homer, Odyssey, 1. 71, 13. 96, 345). The characterization 'old man of the sea' is attributed by Homer to Proteus and Nereus also. As Kereyni points out, it is not possible to distinguish between the three and decide whether they are not but different manifestations of the same deity. Kerenyi (1982) 53.
[68] Hesiod, Theogony 270 ff.
[69] Hesiod, Theogony, 333 ff.
[70] Schol. ad Apollon. Rhod. 4. 1399.

he got Scylla.[71] A fragment of Sophocles (fr. 777) has him as the father of the Sirens, too.[72] The Graeae and the Gorgons are called Phorcids, daughters of Phorcys, so that they are distinguished from other Graeae, old women, such as the three Fates.

Graeae (Γραῖαι)

Despite their name, the Graeae (Γραῖαι, Old Women) are not necessarily wrinkled and aged. In the *Theogony* Hesiod writes, 'Keto gave to Phorcys the Graeae with the beautiful cheeks, who were born with white hair; for this they are called Graeae (Old Women or Grey Ones) by gods and mortals'.[73] On a red-figure crater from the 5th c. B.C., now kept at the Archaeological Museum on the island of Delos, one can see the hero Perseus with his winged sandals walking away from one of the Graeae, looking back at her; she is staring at the opposite direction – perhaps she was the one without the eye. This Graea has the form of an ordinary woman, and this is why she is included here in the category of humanoid monsters. However, in the 5th c. BC, the playwright Aeschylus had written a play entitled *Phorcides*, part of a trilogy on the life of Perseus, in which the Phorcides constituted the chorus. For Aeschylus, the Graeae were monsters like the sirens, with the head and arms of old women and the bodies of swans. As many an instance in Greek myth, versions of the same stories vary as much and as tremendously as the shape and characteristics of the same monsters.

Their number varies. Hesiod names two of them, ‹the grey sisters, Pemphredo robed in beauty and Enyo robed in saffron›.[74] Aeschylus raises their number to three.[75] The third sister is called either Persis (Περσίς, Destroyer) or Deino (Δεινώ, Fearsome, Terrible).[76]

According to Kerenyi, Enyo is a warlike name and it would be fitting for a goddess of battle. Therefore she is closely associated with Ares, the god of war and often accompanies him in battle – an image found often in the epics of Homer.[77]

---

[71] Schol. on Apollonius 4. 828; Eustathius, ad Homerum, p. 1714; Tzetzes, ad Lycophron 45. Schol. on Odyssey 124, claims that her mother was also called Lamia.

[72] Since the Sirens are hybrids (half man or woman and half bird, they are discussed in chapter 3.

[73] Hesiod, Theogony 270 ff. The Graeae with the white hair may be a personification of the beautiful, ageless white waves of the sea and the sea-god Phorcys.

[74] Hesiod, Theogony 270ff.

[75] Aeschylus, Prometheus 793.

[76] Apollodorus, The Library, 2.4. 2; Pseudo-Hyginus, Preface: 'From Phorcus and Ceto: Phorcides Pemphredo, Enyo and Persis (for this last others say Dino)'.

[77] Homer, Iliad, 5. 333, 592. Pausanias (Description of Greece, 4.30.5) writes that Homer represented Athena and Enyo as supreme in war.

And with him followed the Trojan battalions in their strength; and Ares led them with the goddess Enyo, carrying with her the turmoil of shameless hatred.[78]

The same idea prevails in the 5th c. B.C. In his *Seven Against Thebes*, Aeschylus presents Enyo as a sanctifier of warlike oaths for the warriors that march against the city of Oedipous:

Seven warriors, fierce regiment-commanders, slaughtered a bull over a black shield [before the commencement of battle], and then touching the bull's gore with their hands they swore an oath by Ares, by Enyo, and by Phobos (Rout) who delights in blood, that either they will level the city and sack the Kadmeans' town by force, or will in death smear this soil with their blood.[79]

This is an image so powerful that was preserved until late antiquity and made a strong impression on epic poets like Quintus Smyrnaeus (4th c. A.D.). His epic *Fall of Troy* is filled with descriptions of battle scenes imitating Homeric style and Enyo appears prominently in these lines.

The black Keres (Fates) joyed to see their conflict [the Greeks and the Trojans], Ares laughed, Enyo yelled horribly. With corpses earth was heaped, with torrent blood was streaming: Eris (Strife incarnate) o'er the slain gloated.[80]

Enyo is closely associated with the turmoil of battle, that the absence of Enyo is a sign of peace and neutrality. In describing the peaceful, sacred island of Delos, the birth place of Apollo and Artemis, Callimachus (3rd c. B.C.) underlines the connection of Enyo with Death and War.

There, [i.e. the island of Delos] treads not Enyo, not Hades, nor the horses of Ares.[81]

Pausanias (2nd c. A.D.) describes a temple of Athens with a statue of Enyo, sculpted by Praxiteles, standing next to the statue of Ares.[82] The lexicon of *Suidas* describes a festival called *Homonoia* (reconciliation) at Thebes and Orchomenos of

---

[78] Homer, Iliad, 5. 590 ff.
[79] Aeschylus, Seven Against Thebes, 41 ff. (transl. Smyth).
[80] Quintus Smyrnaeus, Fall of Troy, 11. 151ff. Also, Fall of Troy 1. 365 ff, 2. 25, ff, 525 ff, 8. 186 ff, 286 ff, 424 ff, 11. 7 ff, 151 ff, 237 ff, 12. 436 ff, 13. 85 ff. Similar descriptions in the works of the 3rd c. A. D. Greek orator Philostratus the Elder (Imagines, 2. 29): We see in the plain corpses upon corpses, and horses lying as they fell, and the arms of the warriors as they slipped from their hands, and this mire of gore in which they say Enyo delights.
[81] Callimachus, Hymn 4 to Delos, 275 ff.
[82] Pausanias, 1. 8, 5.

Boeotia. It was held in the honour of Zeus, Demeter, Athena and Enyo. Zeus was addressed with the adjective Homoloius, after the name of the priestess of Enyo, Homolois.[83]

Pemphredo is associated with the wild bee, according to Kerenyi.[84] However, the name Πεμφρηδώ means *the one who shows the way*, the *leader* and she must have got her name due to the role she played in the story of Perseus, as she is the one who showed him the way to the land of the Gorgons, where the hero slew Medusa.

Their monstrous appearance consists in them having only one eye and one tooth in common, which they borrow from each other. Such a characteristic is not attributed to them by Homer or the earlier descriptions. Later writers located them under mount Atlas,[85] or 'somewhere beyond India'.[86] In earlier tradition, they live outside Greece, in the East, most probably beyond 'the stream that bounds the two continents' (perhaps the Red Sea). This is what we are informed by Prometheus, when he advises hapless cow-shaped Io to steer off the country or the Gorgons (Gorgonean plains of Cisthene). In Aeschylus' *Prometheus Bound* the three daughters of Phorcys are described as *kyknomorphoi*, swan-shaped, but this should not necessarily allude to some hybrid form; it could just be a description of a beautiful figure, just like that of a swan.

> When you have crossed the stream that bounds two continents press on, over the surge of the sea, toward the east where the sun stalks in flame, to the Gorgonean land, Kisthene (Cisthene). There live Phorkys' (Phorcys') aged virgin daughters, in shape like swans, possessing one eye and one tooth between the three; beings on whom no ray of sun ever looks down, nor moon at night. And close to them their three winged sisters . . . the snake-haired Gorgones.[87]

Tradition popularizes them after the 5th c. B.C., after their encounter with Perseus. From goddesses of war, myth now turns them into guardians of the Gorgons. They are the only ones who know where the Gorgons live and Perseus must force them to tell him their secret.

Perseus managed to steal their eye, as they were passing it from one to another, and thus forced them to tell him where the Gorgons lived.

---

[83] Suid. s. v.; comp. Müller, Orchom. p. 229, 2nd edit.
[84] Kerenyi (1982) 56. In the Homeric hymn to Hermes they appear as bees.
[85] Ovid, Metamorphoses, 4. 770ff.
[86] Nonnus, Dionysiaca, 31. 13.
[87] Aeschylus, Prometheus Bound, 791ff.

The story of Perseus is one of the most popular in the rich tradition of Greek mythology. Wondrous deeds, gods, monstrous creatures, famous offsprings[88] and descendants that reach the even more popular Hercules; thus he is the founder of the royal family of Mycenae in the Peloponnese and a forefather even of the Persians.[89] He is the child of mortal Danae and powerful Zeus.[90] Everything begins long ago in the city of Argos. The fifty daughters of king Danaus[91] flee away from Egypt, because they do not want to forcibly marry their cousins, the fifty sons of their uncle, Egyptus. In a story dramatized by the 5th c. B.C. playwright Aeschylus (the Danaid trilogy, from which only the *Suppliants* survives), the daughters of Danaus return to their ancestral land, Argos, as suppliants. However, in order to avoid implicating the city in imminent war with the Egyptians who pursue them, they agree to marry their cousins, only to kill them during their wedding night,

---

[88] One of his famous sons is Sthenelus (Homer, Iliad, 19. 97; Apollodorus, 2. 49). After he rescued Andromeda from the sea monster, he also got Perses, Alcaeus, Helius, Mestor, Electryon and Gorgophone. Pausanias (3.1.4, 3.2.4, 2.21.7) mentions also Gorgophone and Kynouros (3.2.2). Electryon is mentioned by Diodorus Siculus, 4. 91. 1).

[89] Herodotus, Histories, 7. 61. 1: They [the Persians] were formerly called by the Greeks Kephenes, but by themselves and their neighbours Artaei. When Perseus, son of Danae and Zeus had come to Kepheus son of Belos and married his daughter Andromeda, a son was born to him whom he called Perses, and he left him there; for Cepheus had no male offspring; it was from this Perses that the Persians took their name. Also, Herodotus, Histories, 7.150. 1-3: There is a story told in Hellas that before Xerxes set forth on his march against Hellas, he sent a herald to Argos, who said on his coming (so the story goes), `Men of Argos, this is the message to you from King Xerxes. Perses our forefather had, as we believe, Perseus son of Danae for his father, and Andromeda daughter of Kepheus for his mother; if that is so, then we are descended from your nation. In all right and reason we should therefore neither march against the land of our forefathers, nor should you become our enemies by aiding others or do anything but abide by yourselves in peace. However, Herodotus cautions towards the interpretation of the opposite side: but the Persian tale is that Perseus himself was an Assyrian, and became a Greek, which his forebears had not been; the Persians say that the ancestors of Akrisios had no bond of kinship with Perseus, and they indeed were, as the Greeks say, Egyptians (Herodotus, Histories, 6. 54. 1).

[90] Homer, Iliad, 14. 319; Pindar, Pythian 12. 16; Apollodorus 2. 34; Strabo 10. 5. 10; Herodotus 6. 53, 7. 61; Didorus Siculus 4. 9. 1; Hyginus, Fabulae 63, 155; Ovid, Metamorphoses, 4. 607; Nonnus, Dionysiaca 2. 286.

[91] He got them by ten different wives, named Atlantie, Elephantis, Erse, Europe, Crino, Memphis, Pieria, Polyxo, Phoebe and an anonymous Aethiopian girl. Strabo calls them Danai (8. 371) and Ovid calls them Velids, after their grandfather Belus (Ovid, Metamorphoses 4. 463). After the death of Belus, they followed their father away from Libya in fear of their uncle Egyptus. Initially, they stopped at the island of Rhodes, where three of them stayed back for ever at Lindos (Diodorus, 5. 58)

after their father's advice.⁹² Only one daughter, Hypermestra, spares her husband, Lynceus, because he respected her decision to remain a virgin. She and Lynceus got two sons, Acrisius and Proetus. As often found in myths,⁹³ the two heirs are supposed to rule Argos in common. However, they had been fighting, even unborn in their mother's belly. Pausanias reports of a tomb made of shields, on the way from Argos to Epidaurus, where the two brothers dueled – it was there where the round shields were invented.⁹⁴ After this, Acrisius and Proetus decided to separate their rule and they became kings in the strong Peloponnesian cities of Argos and Tiryns, respectively.

Initially, Proetus went off to Asia Minor, married Stheneboia, princess of Lycia (known mostly for her love of Bellerophon) and returned to Tiryns. Seven Cyclopes came to his aid and helped him build the immense fortification of the city.⁹⁵ As for Acrisius, he had no children, and sent for advice at the oracle of Delphi. The answer of the Pythia did not please him. She foretold that he would get a daughter, and her son would kill him. Acrisius built an underground jail of bronze or stone and shut his daughter in there, so that she would never come in contact with men.⁹⁶ This did not deter Zeus, who transformed himself into golden rain and came down on her through the grids of her jail and impregnated her.⁹⁷ When Acrisius found out that despite his precautions Danae had given birth to a son, he took mother and child and enclosed them in a chest and had it thrown into the sea, hoping that they would not perish by his own hand. The waves brought the chest to the small island of Seriphos, in the Cyclades. A fisherman called Diktys (Δίκτυς, the one who uses the net) pulled the chest out of the sea.⁹⁸

Diktys might be a fisherman, but his brother⁹⁹ is the local king, Polydectes (Πολυδέκτης, the one who receives a lot, or many). Now tradition becomes so diverse that it is difficult to conclude on a commonly accepted version.¹⁰⁰ One

---

⁹² For this they were punished in the afterlife by eternal torture: they had to carry water with a jug full of holes, so that it always leaked. The phrase Δαναΐδων πίθος, 'water jug of the Danaids', remained proverbial and signified any futile task.
⁹³ Like the children of Oedipus, Eteocles and Polynices who should have shared power after their father's exile.
⁹⁴ Pausanias, 2. 25. 7.
⁹⁵ Strabo, 8. 6. 11.
⁹⁶ Soph. Ant. 947; Lycoph. 838; Horat. Carm.3. 16
⁹⁷ This is why some writers attributed the adjective χρυσόπατρος (of a golden father) to him. Cf. Lycophron, 838; Ovid, Metamorphoses, 250.
⁹⁸ Dramatized in the satyr-play Diktyoulkoi (net fishermen) by Aeschylus in the fifth c. B.C., from which only some verses have survived.
⁹⁹ Schol. on Apollonius Rhodius 4. 1091.
¹⁰⁰ Latin sources present a totally different version. According to Virgil, the chest was carried

version of the story has Polydektes taking Danae as a slave at the palace.[101] Others say that she married Polydektes.[102] In most cases, the king courts Danae, who is protected by her son and the king tried to get rid of him, by sending him to fetch the head of the Gorgon Medusa, the only Gorgon who was mortal, in order to give it as a wedding present to Hippodameia.[103]

Perseus would not have succeeded without the aid of the gods. Hermes and Athena are on his side. Some sources say that it was Hermes who appeared to him first.[104] Who else could have given him the flying sandals that enabled him to leave the island and escape the Gorgons, but Hermes?[105] Eratosthenes in his work *Katasterismoi* claims that Aeschylus wrote the same detail in his *Phorcides*.[106] In any case, to overcome monstrous creatures, one must be equipped with extraordinary gear. Athena advised him to find the Graeae, who knew not only the residence of Medusa, but also that of the Nymphs, the three mystical women in possession of magical weapons needed, to complete this seemingly impossible task.

The nymphs willingly helped Perseus and gave him three valuable accessories to overcome the Gorgons. According to later tradition, it was they and not Hermes who gave Perseus the winged sandals, and also a bag to store the head of Medusa once it was cut off, and a cap or helmet of Hades that made him invisible. Hermes also gave him a sickle to cut off the head and Athena gave him a mirror, so that he would not gaze directly at Medusa lest he turned into stone.[107] Thus armed,

---

to the coast of Italy, where king Pilumnus married Danaë, and founded Ardea (Virg. Aeneid vii. 410; Serv. ad Aeneid vii. 372); or Danaë is said to have come to Italy with two sons, Argus and Argeus, whom she had by Phineus, and took up her abode on the spot where Rome was afterwards built (Serv. ad Aeneid viii. 345). A different version has Polydectes marrying Danae, and Perseus was brought up in the temple of Athena. Acrisius found out and he went to Seriphos, but Polydectes stood on Perseus' side. The young hero promised not to kill his grandfather. However, storms broke out, and Acrisius had to stay at Seriphos with his fleet. During that time Polydectes died. As was accustomed, funeral games were held to honour him. Perseus threw the discus, but the wind carried it and it struck the head of Acrisius, and killed him, whereupon Perseus proceeded to Argos and took possession of the kingdom of his grandfather (Hyginus. Fabulae, 63).

[101] Pindar, Pythian 12. 15.
[102] Hyginus, Fabulae, 63.
[103] Tzetzes, ad Lycophron 838.
[104] Schol. on Apollonius Rhodius, Argonautica 4. 1515.
[105] Kerenyi (1983) 301.
[106] Eratosthenes, Katasterismoi, 22.
[107] Hes. Scut. Her. 220, 222; Eurip. Elect. 460; Anthol. Palat. ix. 557; comp. Hygin. Poet. Astr. ii. 12; Theon, ad Arat. p. 29.

Perseus flew off to Kisthene, the island of the Gorgons in the Red Sea, between Africa and Arabia.

> As Aeschylus, the writer of tragedies, says in his 'Phorcides', the Graeae were guardians of the Gorgones. We wrote about them in the first book of the 'Genealogiae'. It is said that they shared one eye, and thus they kept watch taking turns. This is the eye that Perseus snatched, as one of the Gorgons was passing it to another, and he threw it in Lake Tritonis. Thus, when the guardians were blinded, he easily killed the Gorgon when she was overcome with sleep.[108]

The same account is recorded by Nonnus in his *Dionysiaca*:

> He [Perseus] laid ambush for the sentinel eye of Phorkys (Phorcys), the ball of the sleepless eye that passed from hand to hand, giving each her share under the wing of sleep in turn.[109]

The three old sisters were thus forced to help Perseus. According to some versions the eye and tooth were returned to them once they told him what he wanted, but as we saw in Pseudo-Hyginus' text, some believed that the eye was thrown into lake Tritonis, in Libya. The same version is accounted by Aeschylus in a lost tragedy called *The children of Phorcys*.[110]

Gorgons (Γοργόνες)

Besides the aforementioned Phorcys and Keto, the ancestry of Medusa is not clear. Hyginus (2nd c. A.D.) reports in his *Fabulae* that Medusa was the daughter of Echidna and an ancient Gorgon: *From Typhon the giant and Echidna were born Gorgon ... Medusa, [was] daughter of Gorgon*.[111] It seems that there is some confusion with a Gorgon named Aix, a daughter of the sun god Helios, killed by Zeus. She seems to be of indeterminable gender, or she had a terrible, perhaps bearded face.[112]

A very ancient depiction of Perseus cutting off the head of Medusa, on an archaic Boeotian vase, now in the Louvre, shows her as a creature half-woman and half horse. Kerenyi (1982, pp. 300-301) says that this is in accordance with a version of Perseus' story. Perseus claimed the beautiful princess Hippodamea, daughter of Oenomaus. King Polydectes had organized a fund for her, and poor Perseus, raised

---

[108] Pseudo-Hyginus, Astonomica 2. 12 (transl. Syropoulos).
[109] Nonnus, Dionysiaca, 25. 64 ff.
[110] March (2014) 210.
[111] Hyginus, Fabulae, 151.
[112] Hyginus, Astronomica, 2. 13.

by a fisherman could offer no wonderful present. Spurred by pride, he promised something rare on a fishermen's island: a horse. The horse that he promised was a mare that had the form of Gorgo, the sight of which literally petrified everyone. The half-woman half-horse image did not seem to catch on. Neither literary descriptions of the Gorgons nor their depictions in art repeat the horse form.

The version of the hybrid Medusa could also be inferred from a later version of the myth, according to which Medusa was once a beautiful girl, unfortunate enough to attract the lustful eye of Poseidon. Apollodorus suggested that Medusa had once dared to compare her beauty with that of Athena and the spiteful goddess deformed her.[113] The Latin poet Ovid spiced up the story by stressing that her hair was particularly beautiful. Poseidon desired her and had intercourse with her in a temple of Athena. Prudent Athena could not punish the god, but she turned Medusa's beautiful hair into fearful snakes.[114]

As already mentioned, Io was warned by Prometheus to stay clear of the land of the Cisthene, where the Graeae and the Gorgons live. [115]

Near them [the Graeae] (live) three winged
snake-haired Gorgons who hate men;
no mortal who has set eyes upon them, still breathes.[116]

The strange element about them is the snake-hair, the protruding tusks and the fact that people die if they see them. Besides these, their bodies are those of normal women, although in early art they are often depicted winged.

Stheno and Euryale sensed what had happened and started pursuing him – a theme very popular in Athenian vase paintings of about 425 B.C. However, they could not see Perseus who was still invisible. They returned to their cave to mourn their sister. The poet Pindar tells us that it was their lament that gave to the goddess Athena the idea of the mournful sound of the *aulos*, the double pipe.[117] The head of Medusa ended up in the hands of Athena. When Perseus offered it to her, she put it onto her primitive armor-plate, a goat skin called *aegis*, which is often depicted decorated with snakes all around it. Sometimes the head of Medusa is shown on the shield of Athena, which thus changed from a defensive means to a formidable offensive weapon against her enemies.

---

[113] Apollodorus, Library 2.4.2-3, 3.10.3.
[114] Ovid, Metamorphoses 4.614-20, 770-803.
[115] Aguirre Castro (1998) 22-31.
[116] Aeschylus, Prometheus Bound, 798-800 (transl. Syropoulos).
[117] Pindar, Pythian 12.6-27.

Gorgon Medusa, Athenian red-figure amphora C5th B.C., Staatliche Antikensammlungen

The blood of Medusa, like the poison of snakes itself, was considered to be both harmful and healing. Drops of her blood fell on the ground and became snakes, which still abound in Libya. Later the Argonaut Mopsus would kill one of these.[118] In Euripides' 5th c. B.C. tragedy *Ion*, it is described how Erichthonius[119] was given two drops of Medusa's blood by Athena. One of them was poisonous and the other

---

[118] Mopsus, son of Ampyx, was a Lapith who fought bravely against the Centaurs during the wedding of Peirithous. He could explain the flight of birds and foretell the future, so the Argonauts took him with them on their journey to Colchis and the quest for the Golden Fleece. On their return, they stopped at Libya, where a snake bit him. Mopsus died and he was buried there. Hesiod, Shield of Hercules 181; Apollodorus, Argonautica 1.65-6, 1080-1106, 4.1502-36; Pausanias 5.17.10; Ovid, Metamorphoses 8.316. 12.455-8.

[119] The fifth mythical king of Athens. Euripides, Ion 20-4, 260-74; Apollodorus 3.14.6; Pausanias 1.2.6, 1.14.6, 1.18.2, 1.24.7, 1.27.2, 3.18.3; Ovid, Metamorphoses 2.552.65.

one was medicinal and had healing powers.[120] The healer son of Apollo, Asclepius, who later became a god, was also in possession of Medusa's blood-drops. Veins from Medusa's left side carried blood that was deadly, but the blood that came from veins of her right side had the power to bring someone back from the dead.

The averting powers of Medusa's dead body also endowed her hair. Later mythographers toyed with the idea of Medusa's head decorated with real hair, too. It is said that a lock of Medusa's hair was given to Hercules by goddess Athena – although Medusa is not named specifically; the lock is described as being of the Gorgons. Hercules kept it in a bronze jar and later gave it to Sterope, daughter of Cepheus, king of Tegea in Arcadia. Hercules wanted to secure Cepheus' assistance at an expedition against the king of Sparta, Hippocoon, but Cepheus did not want to leave Tegea unguarded. Hercules convinced them by entrusting the jar with the Gorgon's lock of hair to Sterope and advised her to hold it up three times while standing on the walls of the city, to turn any approaching enemy to flight. The advice was useful: Tegea was saved, only Cepheus was killed at the battle of Sparta.[121]

Ancient writers tried to rationalize the myth of the Gorgons. To most of them, monstrous creatures with wings and petrifying eyes were hard to believe in. Pausanias and Diodorus attributed warlike bravery and valor to tribes that the Greeks had encountered, perhaps 'wild men and wild women', as Pausanias wrote. These people fought so fiercely that they amazed the Greek warriors and inspired stories about snaky or curly-haired female adversaries. Pausanias writes:

> Not far from the building in the market-place of Argos is a mound of earth, in which they say lies the head of the Gorgon Medousa. I omit the miraculous, but give the rational parts of the story about her. After the death of her father, Phorkys, she reigned over those living around Lake Tritonis, going out hunting and leading the Libyans to battle. On one such occasion, when she had encamped with an army against the forces of Perseus, who was followed by selected troops from Peloponnesos, she was assassinated by night. Perseus, admiring her beauty even in death, cut off her head and carried it to show the Greeks. But Prokles, the son of Eukrates, a Carthaginian, thought a different account more plausible than the preceding. It is as follows. Among the incredible monsters to be found in the Libyan desert are wild men and wild women. Prokles affirmed that he had seen a man amongst them who had been brought to Rome. So he guessed that a woman wandered from them, reached Lake Tritonis, and harried the neighbours

---

[120] Euripides, Ion 989-1017.
[121] Apollonius, Argonautica 1.161-71; Apollodorus 1.8.2, 1.9.16, 2.7.3; Pausanias 8.47.5.

until Perseus killed her; Athena was supposed to have helped him in this exploit, because the people who live around Lake Tritonis are sacred to her.[122]

Following the same line of thought, a very cautionary Diodorus reports in his *Library of Histories*:

> Now there have been in Libya a number of races of women who were warlike and greatly admired for their manly vigour; for instance, tradition tells us of the race of the Gorgones, against whom, as the account is given, Perseus made war, a race distinguished for its valour; for the fact that it was the son of Zeus, the mightiest Greek of his day, who accomplished the campaign against these women, and that this was his greatest labour which may be taken by any man as proof of both the pre-eminence and the power of the women we have mentioned. Furthermore, the manly prowess of those of whom we are now about to write presupposes an amazing pre-eminence when compared with the nature of the women of our day. [Diodorus then goes on to describe a legendary tribe of Libyan Amazon-women.][123]

The story of the Gorgons overcome by Perseus was popular in art throughout antiquity and in many places outside Athens. Besides the numerous vase paintings, statues and reliefs, Pausanias describes a relief in the *Bronze House* of the temple of Athena, giving their gifts to Perseus,[124] a sculpture of Perseus after the beheading of Medusa, by Myron,[125] a relief with the exploits of Bellerophontes against the Chimaera and Perseus who has cut off the head of the Medusa,[126] a relief depicting Perseus killing Medusa at the throne of Apollo at Amyklai in Lacedaemon,[127] and a beautiful relief at the chest of Cypselos at Olympia, showing the two sisters of Medusa chasing Perseus who is flying off with the head of the Medusa. 'Only the name of Perseus is inscribed on him', reports Pausanias.[128]

---

[122] Pausanias, Guide to Greece, 2.21.5-6.
[123] Diodorus, Library of History, 3.52.4 (transl. Oldfather).
[124] Pausanias, 3.17.3.
[125] Pausanias, 1.23.7.
[126] Pausanias, 2.27.2.
[127] Pausanias, 3.18.11.
[128] Pausanias, 5.18.5.

Chapter 2
Serpentine Creatures

Hissing and unfolding their coils stealthily, mostly hidden from one's gaze until it is too late, snakes curdle the blood in most people's veins. Venomous and silent, eerie and creepy, they constitute eternal paradigms of otherness, fascinating imagination and verging from the dangerous to the sacred. We often find them associated with rituals or serving as guardians of sacred items,[129] but more often they represent danger. As part of a creature's form, they can enhance monstrosity. One needs only to recall the snakes that decorated the head of Medusa instead of hair, the serpent tail of the three-headed dog of Hades, Cerberus, and the snake that grew off the back of the hideous Chimaera. Of course, snakes can be scary enough just being themselves; especially when they are larger than usual and equipped with strong teeth and unnatural powers.

Amphisbaena (Αμφίσβαινα)

Amphisbaena has secured a place amongst the bestiary of monsters by the 5th c. B.C. since we find her used as a measure of monstrosity, enhancing the image of the terrible woman Clytemnestra, who killed her husband, Agamemnon, in order to avenge the killing of their daughter by his hands:

> *Such boldness has she, a woman to slay a man. What odious monster shall I fitly call her? An Amphisbaena? Or a Scylla, tenanting the rocks, a pest to mariners, [1235] a raging, devil's mother, breathing relentless war against her husband?*

Aelian is responsible for the description of some of the most fabulous creatures to be encountered in Greek mythology. One of the most unusual is Amphisbaena (from the verb βαίνω, *to go*, and αμφί, *both ways*). He describes it as 'a snake with two heads, one at the top and one in the direction of the tail. When it advances, as need for a forward movement impels it, it leaves one end behind to serve as tail, while the other is used as a head. Then again, if it wants to move backwards, it uses

---

[129] Like the monstrous serpent that guards the golden apples at the garden of the Hesperides: 'And Ceto was joined in love to Phorcys and bore her youngest, the awful snake who guards/] the apples all of gold in the secret places of the dark earth at its great bounds. This is the offspring of Ceto and Phorcys'. Hesiod, Theogony, 334-5 (transl. Evelyn-White). A similar guardian is also the snake that guards the golden fleece at Colchis, and it is overcome by Jason (see Apollodorus, Argonautica).

A 15th-century amphisbaena on a misericord in Buckinghamshire

both heads in exactly the opposite manner than before.'[130] Drawing from an earlier source, Nicander claims that the skin of Amphisbaena 'wrapped round a walking stick drives away all snakes and other creatures, which kill not by biting but by striking'.[131]

More magical qualities of this creature's blood are described by the 1st c. B.C. historian Diodorus Siculus. Although he does not describe an amphisbaena but an *amphisbaena-like* creature, most probably a kind of tortoise, his description is indicative of the potencies that were ascribed to animals that were extraordinary. The creature he describes is one of the many that inhabit the seven isles of the Indian Ocean: 'There are also animals among them, we are told, which are small in size but the object of wonder by reason of the nature of their bodies and the potency of their blood; for they are round in form and very similar to tortoises, but they are marked on the surface by two diagonal stripes, at each end of which they have an eye and a mouth; consequently, through seeing with four eyes and using as many mouths, yet they gather their food into their gullet, and down this its nourishment is swallowed and it all flows together into one stomach; and in like manner its other organs and all its inner parts are single. It also has, beneath it all around its body many feet, by means of which it can move in whatever direction

---

[130] Aelian, On Animals 9.23.
[131] Aelian, On Animals 8.8.

it pleases. And the blood of this animal, they say, has a marvelous potency; for it immediately glues any living member that has been severed in its place; even if a hand or the like should happen to have been cut off, by the use of this blood it is glued on again, provided that the cut is fresh, and the same thing is true of those other parts of the body which are not connected with the regions which are vital and sustain the person's life'.[132]

Nicander, a writer from Colophon who flourished around 130 B.C., was the author of a work in dactylic hexameter entitled *Theriaca*, in which he described various poisonous animals and the antidotes to their poison. He also wrote *Alexipharmaca*, in which he referred to poisons in general, analyzing 19 of them and provided remedies for their treatment.[133] This is the oldest surviving extant work on poison (the word *alexipharmacon* means antidote to poison).[134] Remedies for snake-bite include a prophylactic (98ff), consisting of the flesh of mating snakes, stag's marrow, wax, rose and olive oil to be applied to the skin; root of centaury (500ff), a bitter herb named after the centaur, Chiron, who was supposed to have used it to cure himself of a poisonous wound; as well as a general panacea (935ff) compounded of more than two dozen ingredients. The remedial potencies of the strange animal are described in *Theriaca* 372-380.

In *Natural History*, Pliny the Elder dedicates one of its chapters to 'Different kinds of Serpents'. He describes it thus: 'The amphisbæna has two heads, that is to say, it has a second one at the tail, as though one mouth were too little for the discharge of all its venom.'[135]

The strange snake is mentioned also by Lucan:[136] 'The dangerous amphisbæna, that moves on at either of its heads.'[137]

Finally, in the 5th c. A. D. the epic writer Nonnus described the legendary necklace of the goddess Harmonia.[138] He describes the two-headed Amphisbaina (Amphisbaena) unfolding its coils and spiting her poison from either mouth, rolling with double-gliding motion, and having the heads meeting up as she crawls and jumps in wave-like motion sideways: so that magnificent necklace twisted shaking its crooked back, with its pair of curving necks, which came to meet at the

---

[132] Diodorus Siculus, Library of History, 2.58.2-4 (transl. Oldfather).
[133] On Nicander, cf. Gow, A. S. F. & Scofield A. F., Nicander: The Poems and Poetical Fragments, 1953; Gow, A. S. F. & Scofield A. F., Nicander: The Poems and Poetical Fragments, 1953.
[134] It seems to have been a rather popularizing work, thought to derive from Apollodorus who wrote about poisons in the early 3rd c. B.C. Cicero says that Nicander wrote 'with distinction on rural affairs, using something of a poet's skill,' De Oratore, I.16.69.
[135] Pliny the Elder, Natural History 8.35.
[136] Marcus Annaeus Lucanus, 39 – 65 A.D. Roman writer born in Cordoba
[137] Lucan, ii. ix. 1. 719.
[138] Nonnus, Dionysiaca 5.145-161.

middle, a flexible two-headed serpent thick with scales; and by the curving joints of the work the golden circle of the moving spine bent round, until the head slid about with undulating movement and emitted a hissing sound through the jaws. In front of the two mouths on each side, there, was a golden eagle that seemed to be cutting the open air, upright between the serpent's heads, most probably holding Amphisbaena in it its claws.

Cychreus (Κυχρεύς)

Cychreus is not exactly a snake, or at least, not originally. He is one of the sons of Poseidon and Salamis, the daughter of the river-god Asopus.[139] According to Apollodorus, he became a king of the island of Salamis after killing a serpent. Pausanias claims that Cychreus named the island Salamis after his mother.[140] Since he had no children of his own, he bequeathed the kingdom to Telamon, who had fled to Salamis after having plotted and killed his brother Phocus during an athletic contest.[141]

> ...Telamon went to Salamis, to Cychreus, the son of Poseidon and Salamis, the daughter of Asopus. Cychreus had become king of the island after killing a snake which was ravaging it, and dying childless, left the kingdom to Telamon.[142]

Strabo suggested that the snake was nurtured by Cychreus and it was later driven out by another hero, Eurylochus. The snake fled to nearby Eleusis and became an attendant of the goddess Demeter:

> In the old days [Aegina, the island] had various names, such as Skiras and Cychreia, after some heroes, who remind us on the one hand of the epithet Skiras, which was an attribute to Athena, the name Skira, which was the name given to some small location in Attica, to the religious celebration called Skiros and the month Skirophorion, on the other hand [the epithets remind us] of the Cychreian snake, of which Herodotus talks and which, initially nurtured by the hero Cychreus, was driven out by Eurylochus, because it plagued the island, and found refuge at Eleusis, where Demeter welcomed it and it became her attendant.[143]

---

[139] Asopus was a son of Ocean and Tethys, or of Pero and Poseidon, or of Zeus and Eurynome. Apollodorus, Library, 3. 6.
[140] Pausanias, 1. 35.10.
[141] Apollodorus, Library 3.12.7.
[142] Apollodorus, Library 3.12.7 (transl. Simpson).
[143] Strabo 9.1.9 (transl. Syropoulos).

Cadmus fighting the dragon. Side A of a black-figured amphora from Euboea, ca. 560–550 BC.

Later, Cychreus himself was metamorphosed into a snake. At least this is how he appeared to the Athenians during the naval battle of Salamis in 480 B.C., where the Greeks destroyed the superior Persian fleet.

> *On the island of Salamis - for I come back to what this is about - there is a temple of Artemis and there is also a trophy set for the victory, which was accomplished for the Greeks by Themistocles, son of Neocles. When the Athenians were fighting the Persians at sea, it is said that a dragon appeared at the ships; God gave an oracle, that this had once been the hero Cychreus.*[144]

For this, the Athenians admired him with godlike honors.[145]

---

[144] Pausanias, 1.36.1-6 (transl. Syropoulos).
[145] Plutarch, Theseus 10. 14.

Typhon (Τυφών)

As a child of the mighty Earth, Typhon makes a grandiose appearance in the *Theogony* of Hesiod. He is described as a dragon with the heads of a hundred fire-breathing snakes growing from his shoulders, screaming with all different kinds of voices. He would have become the ruler of mortals and immortals, had it not been for Zeus. The account of Hesiod is mesmerizing:

> When Zeus had driven the Titans from heaven, vast Gaea brought forth the youngest of her children through the love of Tartarus and the agency of golden Aphrodite. The hands of the mighty god were strong in any undertaking and his feet were weariless. From the shoulders of this frightening dragon a hundred snake heads grew, flickering their dark tongues; fire blazed from the eyes under the brows of all the dreadful heads, and the flames burned as he glared. In all the terrible heads voices emitted all kinds of amazing sounds; for at one time he spoke so that the gods understood, at another his cries were those of a proud bull bellowing in his invincible might; sometimes he produced the pitiless roars of a courageous lion, or again his yelps were like those of puppies, wondrous to hear, or at another time he would hiss; and the great mountains resounded in echo.
> Now on that day of his birth an irremediable deed would have been accomplished and he would have become the ruler of mortals and immortals, if the father of gods and men had not taken swift notice and thundered loudly and fiercely; the earth resounded terribly on all sides and as well the wide heaven above, the sea, the streams of Ocean, and the depths of Tartarus. Great Olympus shook under the immortal feet of the lord as he rose up and earth gave a groan. The burning heat from them both, with the thunder and lightning, scorching winds, and flaming bolts reached down to seize the dark-colored sea. The whole land was aboil and heaven and the deep; and the huge waves surged around and about the shores at the onslaught of the immortals, and a quake began its tremors without ceasing.
> Hades who rules over the dead below shook, as did the Titans, the allies of Cronus, in the bottom of Tartarus, from the endless din and terrifying struggle. When Zeus had lifted up the weapons of his might, thunder and lightning and the blazing bolts, he leaped down from Olympus and struck, and blasted on all sides the marvelous heads of the terrible monster. When he had flogged him with blows, he hurled him down, maimed, and vast earth gave a groan. A flame flared up from the god as he was hit by the bolts in the glens of the dark craggy mountain where he was struck down. A great part of vast earth was burned by the immense conflagration and melted like tin heated by the craft of artisans in open crucibles, or like iron which although the hardest of all is softened by blazing fire and melts in the divine earth through the

craft of Hephaestus. Thus the earth melted in the flame of the blazing fire. And Zeus in the rage of his anger hurled him into broad Tartarus.
From Typhoeus arise the winds that blow the mighty rains; but not Notus, Boreas and Zephyr who bring good weather, for they are sprung from the gods and a great benefit for mortals. But the others from Typhoeus blow over the sea at random; some fall upon the shadowy deep and do great harm to mortals, raging with their evil blasts. They blow this way and that and scatter ships and destroy sailors. Those who encounter them on the sea have no defense against their evil. Others blowing over the vast blossoming land destroy the lovely works of mortals born on earth, filling the air with dust and harsh confusion.[146]

So, the monster is defeated by the lightning of Zeus.[147] His legendary battle with Zeus is commemorated in the *Iliad*. Thus, showing that the legendary battle had already been a favored narration and common point of reference to myth-tellers since the time before Homer.

Zeus aiming his thunderbolt at a winged and snake-footed Typhon. Chalcidian black-figured hydria (c. 540–530 BC), Staatliche Antikensammlungen (Inv. 596)

---

[146] Hesiod, Theogony, 820-880 (transl. Morford & Lenardon).
[147] Hesiod, Theogony. 821 ff.

> But the rest went forward, as if all the earth with flame were eaten,   780
> and the ground echoed under them, as if Zeus who delights in thunder
> were angry, as when he batters the earth about Typhoeus,
> in the land of the Arimoi, where they say Typhoeus lies prostrate.[148]

A totally different version concerning the birth of Typhon comes from one of the Homeric Hymns.[149] There it is said that Hera, jealous of Zeus who had given birth to the goddess Athena from his own head, without the participation of a woman, brought forth Typhon on her own, without having consorted with her husband or any other man – this is called *parthenogenesis*. She prayed to Earth for a child that would be stronger than Zeus, striking the ground with her hand, until Earth responded and granted her with what she wanted. Since the child was serpentine (as many children of Earth are), it was given to another snake, Python, to be nurtured.[150] A fragment from the work of the 7th (or 6th c. B.C.) poet Stesichorus, also attests to the parthenogenesis: 'Typhoeus: Hesiod makes him son of Gaia (Earth), Stesichorus son of Hera, who bore him without a father in order to spite Zeus.'[151] The same is written in the *Homeric Hymn to Apollo*:

> She (Echidna) took as foster child from gold-throned Hera   305
> fierce Typhaon, hateful hurt for mankind,
> born out of Hera's rage at Zeus the father,
> when he gave birth to glorious Athena
> from his own head. The lady Hera, furious,
> blurted in the assembly of immortals:
> 'All of you, gods and goddesses, take notice:
> Cloud-gathering Zeus is first to mortify me.
> I was the one he made his honored wife.
> Without me, though, he had grey-eyed Athena,
> shining even among divine immortals.[152]   315

---

[148] Homer, Iliad 2. 780-4 (transl. Lattimore). Cf. Stabo xii, 929 for the information about the land of the Arimoi.
[149] The Homeric Hymns are a collection of thirty-three anonymous Ancient Greek hymns celebrating individual gods. The hymns are 'Homeric' in the sense that they employ the same epic meter—dactylic hexameter—as the Iliad and Odyssey, use many similar formulas and are couched in the same dialect. They were uncritically attributed to Homer from the earliest written reference to them, Thucydides (iii.104).
[150] Homeric Hymn to Apollo 305.
[151] Stesichorus, Frag. 239.
[152] Homeric Hymn to Apollo 305-15(transl. Ruden).

According to Apollodorus (1st c. B.C.), he was born in a cave[153] in Cilicia. 'He was taller than all the mountains and his head touched the stars. If he stretched out his arms, his one hand touched the East and the other the West. His mouth shot forth flames, his body was winged, and from his thighs down he had a mass of huge, coiling serpents'[154] – a description in accordance with popular depiction of Typhon on vase paintings from around the 6th c. B.C. The lyric poet Pindar (6th c. B.C.) also agrees upon the detail of the Cilician cave: 'Typhon the hundred-headed, who long since was bred in the far-famed Kilikion (Cilician) cave'.[155]

In Apollodorus' version, the sight of Typhon rising to the sky against the gods, spitting flames of fire from the mouths of the hundred snakes that covered him, is so frightening that the gods fled to Egypt in terror and changed their forms into animals, to save themselves. Apollo transformed himself into a crow, Hermes into an ibis, Dionysus into a goat, Hercules into a fawn, Hera and Hephaestus into oxen and Leto into a mouse. 'This story was probably invented to explain the animal forms of Egyptian gods who the Greeks identified with Seth, the enemy of Osiris, and Zeus was said to accompany the flight disguised as a ram with curling horns, to account for the cult of Zeus Ammon in ram-shape'.[156]

Only Zeus and Athena were bold enough to face the monster. Zeus attacked him with thunderbolts and pursued him all the way to mount Cassion, at the borders of Egypt and Arabia. There they started a hand-to-hand battle and Zeus wounded the Typhon with a sickle (harpy). Typhon, however, managed to coil himself around the god and cut the sinews of his hands and feet. Weakened and unable to move, Zeus was carried to Corycean Cave at Cilicia. Typhon hid the sinews of Zeus in a bearskin and entrusted it for safekeeping to Delphyne – a monster which was half-girl and halfsnake. Hermes with the aid of Aegipan managed to steal the bearskin and they sewed back the sinews of Zeus. A new relentless chase of Typhon by Zeus began and this time they arrived at Mount Nyssa. There the three Fates tricked Typhon into eating some kind of berries that would, apparently, reinstitute his strength. The chase continued throughout Greece, with Typhon bleeding over the mountain of Thrace, which has ever since then been called Haemos (*haema* meaning 'blood' in Greek). Finally, when they reached Sicily, Zeus threw a whole mountain over Typhon – Mount Aetna. The flames emitted from its top, are nothing but the agonizing fiery breaths of Typhon, who still lies underneath.

---

[153] Apollodorus, Library 1.6.3.
[154] March (2014) 491.
[155] Pindar, Pythian 1.16ff.
[156] March (2014) 492.

Later Roman writers were equally impressed by this story. In the 2nd c. A.D. the mythographer Antoninus Liberalis reported that 'Typhon was the son of Ge (Earth), a deity monstrous because of his strength, and of outlandish appearance. There grew out of him numerous heads and hands and wings, while from his thighs grew huge coils of snakes. He emitted all kinds of roars and nothing could resist his might'.[157]

In the third century A.D., the battle of Typhon and Zeus is still popular, but a new element is added: Pan, a son of Hermes, who helps Zeus to lure the monster and destroy it close to the coast.[158]

Typhon, like all respectable monsters of Greek Myth, was not devoid of paternal instincts. He was considered the father of many other monsters in Greek tradition. By Echidna, he got the Eagle that ate the liver of Prometheus, when he was bound on Mount Caucasus, punished by Zeus for stealing fire from heaven and giving it to mortals: 'When he (Hercules) reached the mainland on the other side he killed the Eagle on Caucasus with an arrow, the offspring of Echidna and Typhon, that had been eating the liver of Prometheus'.[159] Also by Echidna, he was the father of the Sphinx: 'While he (Creon) was king, a great plague held Thebes in suppression, for Hera had sent upon them the Sphinx, whose parents were Echidna and Typhon'.[160] The famous sow of Crommyon, a wild boar killed by Theseus, was also a child of Echidna and Typhon: Theseus slew the sow at Crommyon, named Phaia after the old woman who kept it. Some say its parents were Echidna and Typhon'.[161] The terrible guardian of the underworld, the watchdog Cerberus, was also a child of Typhon and Echidna: 'Cerberus, who Echidna had borne to Typhon in a craggy cave's gloom close to the borders of Eternal Night'.[162] According to Quintus Smyrnaeus, his children were also two terrifying dragons who lived in a cave beneath a cliff near the citadel of Troy: 'A cave was there, beneath a rugged cliff (near Troy) with massive, beyond comparison, fearful monsters living in it, of the deadly line of Typhon'.[163] Hyginus informs us that Typhon and Echidna[164] were also the parents of Gorgon, the father of the Gorgons, Cerberus, the dragon that guarded the apples of the Hesperides, the Hydra of Lerna, later killed by Hercules, the dragon that guarded

---

[157] Antoninus Liberalis, Metamorphoses 28 (transl. Celoria).
[158] Oppian, Halieutica 3.15. Pan was a son of Hermes and Penelope: Schol. Ἑρμοῦ γὰρ καὶ Πηνελόπης ὁ Πᾶν; Hom. H. XIX.1.Ἑρμείαο φίλον γόνον; Plin. VII.204 Pan Mercuri (filius).
[159] Pseudo-Apollodorus, Bibliotheca 2.120. Cf. Pseudo-Hyginus, Astronomica 2.15.
[160] Pseudo-Apollodorus, Bibliotheca 3.52.
[161] Pseudo-Apollodorus, Bibliotheca E1.1.
[162] Quintus Smyrnaeus, Fall of Troy 6.260ff.
[163] Quintus Smyrnaeus, Fall of Troy 12. 444ff.
[164] Nonnus also reports that Typhon was the father of Echidna. Nonnus, Dionysiaca 18.274ff.

the golden fleece at Colchis, later killed by Jason, Scylla, the Sphinx and the terrible Chimaera in Lycia.[165] Even the terrible Harpies, the monstrous birds with women's faces who snatched away the food of the hapless and blind Phineus, were children of Typhon.[166]

Python (Πύθων)

One of the most famous oracles of antiquity is that at the temple of Apollo at Delphi. Stretching its influence beyond the borders of Greece, the temple attracted visitors from all over the ancient world. Based on a well-organized system of informants and international relations, the temple was always able to offer wisely considered advice to those interested; in cases of doubtful situations, the priests would give dubious answers on behalf of the god, who was also known in antiquity by the epithet *loxsias*, 'the obscure'. The ideal location of the temple made it very popular. In fact, it was so popular that before Apollo's arrival, the area was occupied by a monstrous snake: Python.

In the *Homeric Hymn to Apollo* we read about the killing of the huge serpent that dwelled the area where the temple lies today. According to this version, Apollo is not just a slayer of a divine offspring, but he is the rescuer of locals who suffered because of the snake.

> *The endless human nations raised a temple*
> *of carved stone, to be sung about forever.*
> *A lovely spring flowed near. The noble son*
> *of Zeus killed a huge snake with his stout bow there,*
> *a savage, bloated monster, who brought outrage*
> *continually against the country's people*
> *and slender-footed sheep – a gory curse.*[167]

According to this very old version, after Earth had given birth to terrifying Typhon, she gave him to a female dragon, named Python, for nurturing. Apollo killed her and with the help of Helios, the sun, her body dried up and rotted away. The place was named Pytho, after the female dragon, and the same adjective accompanied Apollo for all eternity: Pythian Apollo.[168] The lyric poet Simonides

---

[165] Hyginus, Fabulae 151.
[166] Valerius Flaccus, Argonautica 4.514.
[167] Homeric Hymn to Apollo 298-304 (transl. Ruden).
[168] Homeric Hymn to Apollo, 356ff.

Apollo killing Python. A 1581 engraving by Virgil Solis for Ovid's Metamorphoses, Book I.

adds the detail of Apollo using one hundred arrows to kill her: [Apollo] *killed the snake Python with a hundred arrows*.[169]

In the 2nd c. A.D. Apollodorus informs us that 'Apollo made his way to Delphi, where Themis gave the oracles at that time. When the serpent Python, which guarded the oracle, moved to prevent Apollo from approaching the oracular opening, he slew it and thus took command of the oracle'.[170] The myth changes slightly and Apollo appears as the attacker against a guardian of the sacred place, where a female predecessor of his, named Themis (Justice) offered oracles. Apollo is not new at killing snakes. One of his earliest adventures was the killing of the monster Delphyne who lived in a cave at the slopes of mount Parnassus.[171]

---

[169] Simonides, Fragment 573. It is probable that Simonides is inspired by the epithet hekateros which often accompanies Apollo and it means 'hundred missiles'. Alternative versions are mentioned by Ogden (2013) 44-45.

[170] Apollodorus, Library 1.22.

[171] It was one of the early adventures of Apollo, since Apollonius says that Apollo was still a

According to Suidas (10th c. A.D. Byzantine Lexicon) the sanctuary of Delphi was named after the serpent Delpnyne who lived there and was killed by Apollo.[172]

The killing of Python was not received well by everyone. A lyric poet of the 5th c. B.C. called Melanippides wrote, '[the mythical musician] Olympus was the first to use the Lydian mode, when he played on his pipes a lament for the Python'.[173]

To rationalize a myth like this is not easy. Today, for example, there are theories associating the snake with the dangerous swamps dried up by the sun (Apollo). Fights of gods with snakes are popular in many world cultures (Asia Minor, Mesopotamia, Egypt),[174] and many other gods in Greek myths appear fighting monstrous snakes (Zeus with Typhon, Perseus with the monster of the sea, etc.). Others associate the snake with the worship of ancient deities or daemons that were later replaced by anthropomorphic gods. Analogous efforts of rationalization of the myth were undertaken by the 2nd c. A.D. writer Pausanias:

> *The most widespread tradition [for the naming of Pytho, Phokis] has it that the victim of Apollon's arrows rotted here, and that this was the reason why the city received the name Pytho. For the men of those days used pythesthai for the verb 'to rot'. . . .* [175]*The poets say that the victim of Apollon was a Drakon posted by Ge to be a guard for the oracle. It is also said that he was a violent son of Krios, a man with authority around Euboia. He pillaged the sanctuary of the god, and he also pillaged the houses of rich men. But when he was leading a second expedition, the Delphians besought Apollon to keep away from them the danger that threatened them. Phemonoe, the prophetess of that day, gave them an oracle verse:--'At close*

'beardless youth rejoicing his locks'. Apollonius Rhodius, Argonautica 2.703ff.

[172] Suidas, s.v. Delphi (transl. Suda on Line). Δελφοί: τὸ ἱερὸν τοῦ Ἀπόλλωνος. οὕτω δὲ ἐκλήθη διὰ τὸ τὸν Δελφύνην δράκοντα ἐκεῖ εὑρεθῆναι, ὃν ἀπέκτεινεν ὁ Ἀπόλλων. Πυθὼ δέ, διὰ τὸ ἐκεῖ σαπῆναι. καὶ Δελφίς, ἡ Δελφική, ἡ τοῦ Ἀπόλλωνος. Δελφὶς γὰρ φάμα τόδ' ἐθέσπισεν, ὄφρα γενοίμαν τᾶς κείνου νύμφας σῆμα καὶ ἱστορίη: The sanctuary of Apollo. It was thus named because the serpent Delphyne was found there, the one which Apollo killed.[1] But [sc. it was also called] Pytho, because it rotted there.[2] Also [sc. attested is] Delphis, [meaning] the Delphian [woman], the [priestess] of Apollo.'For the Delphian voice prophesied thus, that I might become the monument and story of his bride.'[3]

[173] Melanippides, Fragment 5 (from Plutarch, On Music). Perhaps the most vivid description of music inspired by the killing of the dragon by Apollo, is described by Strabo (Geography 9.3.10). Strabo describes in great detail the musical composition of Timosthenes, the admiral of the second Ptolemy, who conveyed the spirit of the battle by using different rhythms, musical instruments e.t.c., culminating in 'the expiration of the Dragon as pipes, since with pipes players imitated the dragon as breathing its last hissing'.

[174] Burkert (2013) 18.

[175] Liddel & Scott: πύθω = to make rot, to rot, Il., Hes.:—Pass. to become rotten, to decay, Hom.

> *quarters a grievous arrow shall Apollon shoot at the spoiler of Parnassos; and of his blood-guilt the Kretans shall cleanse his hands' but the renown shall never die.' It seems that from the beginning the sanctuary at Delphoi has been plotted against by a vast number of men. Attacks were made against it by this Euboian pirate.*[176]

The idea of killing a serpent sacred to Gaea was rather disturbing to the ancient mind. Consequently, Apollo had to organize funeral games in honor of Python.[177] In memory of the killing of the snake, the priestess of Apollo, who served as an intermediate between him and the people who came asking for oracles, was always named Pythia.

Pausanias also adds that Python was killed by both Apollo and his twin sister Artemis. After their deed the two gods came to Aigialeia, at Sicyon, to obtain purification from the stain of murder.[178] This is probably a later explanation (1st to 2nd c. A.D.) about the origin of the Pythian Games.

Hydra of Lerna (Λερναία Ὑδρα)

Snakes have traditionally been regarded as either dangerous or guardians of good, just like Hercules. After all one can definitely claim that Hercules is the champion of mankind, the defeater of monsters and the savior of the weak. He is the man who wrestled death to bring back a dead queen (see Euripides' *Alcestis*) and descended to the underworld alive, only to return with the ultimate trophy, Cerberus. However, Hercules is also the man who – unknowingly, since he was driven mad by Hera – killed his own family, mistaking them for enemies (Euripides' *Hercules*); he is however conscious of many other crimes: the killing, even if accidental, of his music teacher, Linus and the deliberate killing of a whole city, so that he could get a woman that he liked: Iole (Sophocles' *Trachiniae*). In one of his oldest appearances in literature, in Homer's *Iliad*, we are reminded of his potentially impious character: it is the Hercules who even attacked Hera and Hades, causing them unbearable pain. This is what we are reminded of by Dione, mother of Aphrodite, according to Homer's version, who recounts cases of immortals attacked by mortals:

> *Hera had to endure*[179] *it when the strong son of Amphitryon* [Hercules] *struck her beside the right breast with a tri-barbed arrow, so that the pain he gave her could not be quieted. Hades*

---

[176] Pausanias, 10.6.5 (transl. Jones).
[177] Photius, Myriobiblon 190.
[178] Pausanias, 2.7.7.
[179] Homer, Iliad 5. 392-402 (transl. Lattimore).

*the gigantic had to endure with the rest of the flying arrow
when this self-same man, the son of Zeus of the aegis,
struck him among the dead men at Pylos, and gave him to agony;
but he went up to the house of Zeus and to tall Olympos
heavy at heart, stabbed through and through with pain, for the arrow
was driven into his heavy shoulder, and his spirit was suffering.
But Paieon* [the doctor of gods], *scattering medicine that still pain,
healed him, since he was not made to be one of the mortals.*

Modern Peloponnese is one of Greece's most attractive areas, blessed with natural beauty and fertile lands. Ancient Lerna was such a place even in antiquity.[180] Many springs and rivers turned the land into a prosperous acquisition for any local ruler. The waters of Lerna were known for their superior quality even in antiquity,

Hercules killing the Hydra of Lerna. Caeretan black-figure hydria (c. 346 BC)

---

[180] Aeschylus, Prometheus Bound 655ff: (Prometheus advises Io)'Do not, my child, spurn the bed of Zeus, but go forth to Lerna's meadow land of pastures deep and to your father's flocks and where his cattle feed, so that the eye of Zeus may find respite from its longings).

as is recorded in Atheneaus, *Deipnosophistae*: 'The dinner being slow in coming, a discussion arose concerning water – which was the sweetest? Some praised the water of Lerna, others, again, the water of Peirene.'[181]

Despite its natural abundance in waters, Lerna was traditionally associated with stories about illness and lack of water as punishment for terrible crimes. In Aeschylus' tragedy *Suppliants*, we learn how the fifty daughters of Danaus fled from Egypt to avoid marrying by force their fifty cousins from Danaus' brother Egyptus. The suppliants arrive at Argos and seek refuge, but when the fifty Egyptians arrive, the Danaids agree to marry them, in order to save the city from imminent war.[182] Their plan is to kill their grooms on their wedding night, according to their father's advice. Forty-nine of them obeyed, but the youngest one, Hypermestra, spared her husband Lynceus, either because she loved him, or because he respected her chastity. Her father brought her to justice for disobedience, but the judges acquitted her. The heads of the unfortunate forty-nine grooms were buried at Lerna, perhaps giving rise to the cursed land that became the lair of the monstrous Hydra. As for the Danaids, some myths record that their father managed to marry them off, not without difficulty, after Hermes had them purified from murder,[183] in other myths they were forever punished in the underworld, fetching – repeatedly – water in jars that were constantly leaking, thus giving birth to a proverb about endless sufferings: the Danaids' Jar.[184]

Another myth associates the area with a common story of gods fighting over the great privilege of being its patrons (like the story of the city of Athens, for the patronage of which Poseidon and Athena were fighting over – a story attested on the Parthenon). This time it is Poseidon and Hera who are burning with the desire of being the protectors of Argos. The tribunal of three river gods, Inachus, Cephisus and Asterion, decided that the great honor would be given to Hera. Gods do not take losing very well. Poseidon, being the ruler of all liquid elements caused a great drought. But everything can be changed with the power of love

---

[181] Athenaeaus, Deipnosophistae 4.156e.
[182] Unfortunately, the two following plays of the trilogy, Egyptians and Danaids, are lost; however, many other accounts allow us to complete the tragic story.
[183] Pindar, Pythian 9.111-116; Nemean 10.1-6; Herodotus 2. 182; Pausanias 2.161.1, 2.1.4-2, 2.20.6-7, 2.21.1-2, 2.37.1-2; Horace, Odes 2.11.21-52.
[184] Ἀπληστία: ἡ ἀδηφαγία. καὶ παροιμία: Ἄπληστος πίθος, ὁ ἐν ᾅδου, ὁ τετρημένος. ἐπὶ τῶν πολλὰ ἐσθιόντων· ἀπὸ τοῦ περὶ τὰς Δαναΐδας μύθου, παρ᾽ ὅσον ἀνιμῶσαι ἐκεῖναι ὕδωρ εἰς πίθον ἔβαλλον. πάσχουσι δὲ περὶ τοῦτον τὸν πίθον αἱ τῶν ἀμυήτων ψυχαί: Gluttony.[1] And [there is] a proverb: 'Insatiable Jar', the one in Hades, the perforated one.[2] In reference to those who eat a lot; from the myth of the Danaids, inasmuch as they drew and poured water into a jar.[3] The souls of the uninitiated suffer in respect of this jar. (From Suda on Line).

(or lust). Amymone, one of the Danaids, looking for water one day, was out in the countryside. Finding time for hunting, she shot a sleeping satyr with her arrows. When the satyr attacked her, Poseidon came to her rescue. One has to infer that the god was more appealing than the satyr, because Amymone yielded to his charms, and her reward was a spring of fresh water, created after the god thrust his trident deep into a rock. The spring was named after Amymone, to commemorate the great service to her country.[185]

The second labor of Hercules brought him to this hapless land, close to the spring of Amymone, only this time the beautiful lake is turned into a swamp.[186] His usurper cousin, Eurystheus, had ordered him to kill an abominable water snake with many – seven or nine – heads, that plagued the area, although the precise number of heads is a matter of controversy among sources.[187] As Daniel Ogden points out, 'the literary and iconographic traditions offer a wide range of numbers. Since the Hydra could replace old heads with multiple new ones – at any rate from the time of Euripides – logic requires that the creature boasted different numbers of heads at various times. It is theoretically possible that the serpent began life with a single head and acquired ever increasing numbers in the course of combats, and there is no compelling evidence for a single-headed Hydra in the mythical tradition proper at any point'.[188] The only other specific information we have about the looks of this water-monster comes from Euripides (*Hercules*, c. 480 B.C.), who describes the Hydra as 'viper-headed'.[189]

According to Hesiod's *Theogony*, the monster was a child of Echidna and Typhon,[190] 'whom the white-armed goddess Hera nourished because of her

---

[185] Amymone was also rewarded with an offspring, her son by Poseidon named Nauplius (Apollodorus, Library 2.1.5).

[186] Strabo, Geography 8.6.2: 'the river Lerna as it is called, bearing the same name as the marsh in which is laid the scene of the myth of the Hydra'.

[187] The number of heads tends to vary from time to time: 'The Hydra is called nine-headed by Alcaeus, fifty-headed by Simonides' (Alcaeus, Fragment 443, from Scholiast on Hesiod's Theogony, transl. Campbell). In Simonides' Fragment 569 (from Servius on Virgil's Aeneid), we are informed that 'the Hydra had one hundred snakes; others say there were nine'. Ovid also tells us that the heads were one hundred (Ovid, Metamorphoses 9.69ff). The same information is found in the Lexicon Suidas (s.v. Hudran Temnein. Servius (on Virgil Aeneid 6.575) ascribed three heads to the monster.

[188] Ogden (2013) 28 and n. 5. In his book – the most recent and complete work on the subject of serpents in Greek Myth -- Ogden presents us with iconographic versions of Hercules fighting a single-headed serpent, but he stresses that there is no reason to identify them with the Hydra.

[189] LIMC 'Herakles' 2037.

[190] Hesiod, Theogony 313ff; Hyginus, Fabulae 151.

quenchless grudge against strong Hercules. Yet, he, Hercules, son of Zeus, of the line of Amphitryon, by design of Athena the spoiler and with help from warlike Iolaus, killed this beast with the pitiless bronze sword'.[191]

The Hydra was a real menace. Foul breath that killed people even if they simply inhaled it, poisonous blood that caused instant death, even if someone cut her and came into contact with it, and terrible snake-heads. According to Apollodorus' extended account, the Hydra was of enormous size, with eight mortal heads and a ninth one in the middle, which was immortal.[192] Hercules arrived at the marshes of Lerna on a chariot, driven by his faithful nephew Iolaus. He found the monster next to the spring Amymone. First, he shot flame-arrows at the beast, to bring her out of her nest. Then he started wrestling with her, but she hung on to him by wrapping herself around one of his feet. His club was useless, although he was protected from her venomous bites by his impenetrable lion-hide. Hercules took his sword instead of the club and started cutting off the serpent heads. According to Ogden, various weapons were mentioned by various sources, although by the 700s the image of Hercules attacking the monster with a sword and Iolaus with a – less heroic – *harpē* (sickle) seems to have been established.[193] To his dismay, he saw two new heads growing in the place of the one that he had chopped off.[194]

Athena, always on his side, advised him to have Iolaus cauterize the stumps of the beheaded serpents using a torch; only then would they not grow back. Hercules thus managed to get rid of the growing snake-heads. The last one, the immortal one, he buried deep under a heavy boulder at the side of the road that runs through Lerna to Elaeus.[195]

During his fight, Hera tried to make things harder for the hero, by sending a big crab from the sea, to bite him on his ankle. He either crushed it under his big foot, or his faithful Iolaus killed it for him.[196] Hera then transformed it into the constellation Cancer.

---

[191] Hesiod, Theogony, 313 (transl. Evelyn-White).
[192] Later writers, such as Ptolemy Hephaestion (book 2, summary from Photius Myriobiblon 190) claim that this head was made of gold. This information comes, apparently, from a writer called Aristonicus Tarentinus.
[193] Ogden (2013) 31.
[194] The same detail is told by Diodorus Siculus, Library of History 4.11.5.
[195] Apollodorus, Library, 2. 77-80.
[196] Plato, Euthydemus 297c. Ogden cites Panyasis Heraclea F8 West = [Erastosthenes] Catasterismi1, Seneca Hercules Oetaeus 67 and Hyginus Astronomica 2.23.1, who suggested that the crab joined the battle out of its own accord, to balace Iolaus in the fight. Ogden (2013) 31.

After Hercules had finished, he dipped the tips of his arrows in the poisonous blood of Lerna, thus making them formidable weapons;[197] a mere touch of these lethal points would mean painful death for the unfortunate who came into contact with it, as the centaur Phollus, and Hercules himself, would find out.[198]

In his chapter, *Interpretations of Greek Mythology* (ed. Jan Bremmer), Walter Burkert argues that the myth of the seven headed monstrous serpent was imported from the East, although we cannot be certain about the reasons that led the story to become native of Argos and specifically the area of Lerna. For Burkert, the element of the crab is indicative of the myth's exotic origin since it appears in earlier eastern traditions:

> *There is clear evidence that the god slaying the seven-headed serpent entered West Semitic literature in the Bronze Age and survived there down to the first millennium; the champion is Baal at Ugarit, but the text describing the exploit recurs nearly word for word in Isaiah's praise of Jahwe. The formula must have been preserved orally, as part of a ritual litany. This still does not tell us how, when and where this motif reached the Greek world. Herakles fighting the hydra appears as a drawing on Boeotian fibulae about 700 B.C. It is not possible to show iconographic dependency on an Eastern model in this case, but for the curious detail that a crab is connected with the scene whereas crabs (or scorpions) appear on the earliest, pre-Sargonic representation. It would be excessively skeptical to deny any connection with the East, where a broad and continuous tradition of the 'seven-headed snake' is established by the documents we have, but the contacts must have taken place at an inaccessible level of oral tales.*[199]

The myth of a nine-headed serpent that plagued a swampy area of the ancient Peloponnese, at times when the agricultural economy relied totally upon the cultivation of fertile, arable lands had traditionally attracted the attention of interpreters.

---

[197] Diodorus Siculus, Library of History 4.11.5; Apollodorus, Library, 2. 77-80.
[198] Ogden (2013) 27. The arrows with the blood of the Hydra were used to kill Nessus, the centaur who attempted to rape Hercules' bride, Deianeira, while carrying her across a flooded river. With his dying breath, Nessus advised Deianeira to keep his poisoned blood (myths do not tell us where she kept it, as the monster was dying in the flooded river) and give it to Hercules if his love for her ever ran out. Unsuspecting Deianeira used the blood to anoint a clean tunic for her husband, after he returned from one of his journeys carrying young Iole with him. Hercules died in agonizing pain, only to be rescued, according to other myths, by Athena, and be led to Olympus where he became immortal. Cf. Sophocles' Trachiniae (5th c. B.C.).
[199] Burkert (2013) 18.

The Lernaean Hydra puzzled the Classical mythographers. Pausanias held that it might well have been a huge and venomous water-snake; but that 'Pisander had first called it many-headed, wishing to make it seem more terrifying and, at the same time, add to the dignity of his own verses' (Pausanias: ii. 37. 4). According to the euhemeristic Servius (on Virgil's Aeneid vi. 287), the Hydra was a source of underground rivers which used to burst out and inundate the land: if one of its numerous channels was blocked, the water broke through elsewhere, therefore Heracles first used fire to dry the ground, and then closed the channels.[200]

Stories about monstrous serpents that are killed so that people can gain access to water are often found in Greek myths and in other traditions, too (e.g. Apollo killing Python next to the spring of Castalia, St. George killing the dragon in Christian tradition). Other writers in antiquity also tried to rationalize the myth of the Hydra. Strabo, in his *Geography*, writes:

And Lake Lerna, the scene of the story of the Hydra, lies in Argeia and the Mycenean territory; and on account of the cleansings that take place in there arose a proverb, 'A Lerna of ills'. Now writers agree that the county has plenty of water, and that, although the city itself lies in a waterless district, it has an abundance of wells. These wells they ascribe to the daughters of Danaus, believing that they discovered them ... but they add that four of the wells not only were designated as sacred but are especially revered, thus introducing the false notion that there is a lack of water where there is an abundance of it'.[201]

Pausanias also attests the information about sacred cleansing ceremonies taking place at Lerna. 'On Mount Crathis (northern Arcadia, bordering Achaia), there is a sanctuary of Artemis Pyronia, and in more ancient days the Argives used to bring fire from this goddess for their Lernaean ceremonies'.[202]

Furthermore, it is definitely the innate duality in a serpent's archetypal form that can be interpreted as positive or negative. 'Sometimes the cosmic serpent is viewed as representative of negative energy, sometimes as positive, and sometimes as providing balance and/or ambivalence. The story of Adam and Eve in the Garden of Eden, of the Bible, portrays the serpent as the deceitful harbinger of

---

[200] Graves (2002) 431.
[201] Strabo, Geography 8.6.8.
[202] Pausanias, Description of Greece 8.15.8. Cf. Pausanias, Description of Greece 2.37.1, where he says that the mysteries were established by Philammon, son of Apollo, or perhaps of Hephaestus, who was the father of Thamyris – the famous singer who lost his sight after an unfortunate competition against the Muses.

consciousness and sin. The connection with deceit may stem from the biological observation that many snakes have a forked tongue, with two ends which point in different directions. Often people will say in English, 'he speaks with a forked-tongue,' a clear reference to the characteristic of deceit.'[203]

Serpents are also associated with chthonic rites and it is possible that in antiquity Lerna was a place where purification rituals took place. Moreover, the defeat of the monster could well stand for a symbolic triumph over death. Finally, the recently founded school of Geomythology[204] associates the myth with ancient lakes of the Argolid plain, which are replenished by a complex underground system of springs and rivers around a main spring. The story of Hydra might stand for the effort of ancient farmers to control the flow of these springs and rivers.[205]

---

[203] Maryboy (2009). For further information about the cosmic serpent see Narby (1999).
[204] The term was introduced by Dorothy Vitaliano, professor of Geology at Indiana University in 1968, to indicate cases where geological phenomena can be associated with mythological narrations. Cf. the collection of papers from the 32nd International Geological Congress on 'Myth and Geology', August 2004: L. Piccardi and W. B. Masse (ed.), *Myth and Geology*, London: Geological Society, 2007.
[205] Mariolakos (1998) 3-4, 101-108. Of course, Homer does not consider Hercules less of a hero than later sources do. In other books of the Iliad he is presented as the beloved son of Zeus (*Iliad* book 19).

Chapter 3
Partly Human

Deviation from the ordinary is often considered as monstrosity. A human bigger than the average man, or more fierce or deformed physically or otherwise, is a monster. A serpent larger than what is common for snakes, sometimes endowed with strange powers, is monstrous. However, there is a category which stands out in the world of the monstrous: hybrids. The 12th c. A.D. Byzantine writer John Tzetzes used the word μιξοθήρ (half-beast) to describe Scylla.[206] When the human form is fused with animal forms, the outcome is extraordinary and perplexing. The confusion of forms and their blending in one single, yet inconceivable and inexplicable whole is more monstrous than any other kind of transgression of norms, since it is bewildering, incomprehensible and utterly scary.

Centaurs (Κένταυροι)

Centaurs are definitely the most marginal of Greek monsters, as they occupy a curiously liminal position in respect to the divide between the rational and the non-rational. Not only because of their looks, partly horse and partly man, but also because their nature is not of one kind only. They are outsiders, living in the forests, the place which is undeniably the *anti-polis*, the opposite of the civilized way of life; and this is mostly how they live: outside of the civilized world, passionately and impulsively, brutally and intensively. However, they have the potential for moral greatness and spiritual superiority, kindness and bravery. In short, they combine conflicting potentials, both in form and in nature. Their stories can be categorized in two mythological cycles, one of them relating them to Thessaly and their battle against Theseus and the other to the Peloponnese and their battles against Hercules.

In art and literature they are always depicted in human form from the waist up, and in horse from the waist down. Their origin is indicative of their savage nature. Their story begins with one of the vilest figures in Greek mythology: Ixion.

The wooded plains of Thessaly are the home of the horse-loving Lapiths. Thessaly was traditionally a horse-breeding area of Greece and some of the finest specimens of the indigenous breeds were probably the core of Alexander the Great's victorious cavalry,[207] especially after the changes in formation and maneuvering

---

[206] Müller (1811) 340.
[207] Hammond (1998) 404-425; Lonsdale, D. J. (2007); Sage, M. M. (1996); Fuller (2004). Cf. Arrian, Alexander's Anabasis 3.16, 7.6

PARTLY HUMAN   61

Centauromachy. Tondo of an Attic red-figure kylix. c. 480 BC

developed by the Thessalian Jason of Pherae.[208] There, people bred horses, rode horses, fought on horses and lived with horses. Rider and beast are imagined as one. It is rather expected, that if a legend about monstrous hybrids constituted of man and horse is to be born, Thessaly should be its cradle.

Ixion was king of the Lapiths. He was of divine origin himself, since Ares was his father (in some versions, his father was Leonteus, or Phlegyas, the fiery son of Ares and Chryse. Other versions mention Antion and Perimele). Ixion was also the father of another evil-doer, Peirithoos, the best friend of Theseus, who had tried to abduct Persephone from the kingdom of Hades.[209] Horses become prominent

---

[208] Lendon, J. E. (2006) 98-101.
[209] In Iliad 14, Zeus confesses to Hera that he was the father of Ixion.

in this story during the wedding of Ixion. He wanted to marry Dia[210] and for this he had to offer his father-in-law a present of great value, as it was accustomed. As he neglected to do so, Dia's father stole some of Ixion's horses. Ixion retaliated by killing Dia's father. He invited him to a feast, but while showing him the preparations for the meat, Ixion pushed Deioneus into the burning charcoals and burned him alive.

The consequences of such terrible conscious acts are never unpunished in Greek myths. Ixion went mad, since no one wanted to undertake the rituals that would purify him from the stain (μίασμα) of murder, because he had desecrated one of the most sacred values: hospitality. Ixion roamed the country like a ghost. No one would address him, or receive him as a guest. Zeus, however, took pity on him. Not only did he bring him to Olympus, but he shared the divine table. Having tasted nectar and ambrosia, Ixion wanted more and he desired Hera. Zeus then created an image of Hera out of clouds, *nephelae*, which was appropriately called Nephele. Ixion was tricked into coupling with it and from this union a man named Centaurus was born.[211] According to Pindar, Centaurus mated with the mares of Magnesia on Mount Pelion and they gave birth to the monstrous Centaurs,[212] who were 'like the mother below, the father above'.[213] As for Ixion, in the afterlife, he was punished by suffering eternal martyrdom. According to Pindar, Zeus ordered Hermes to tie him on a wheel of fire and wings, which was eternally spinning across the skies.[214] The condensed account of Apollodorus is very eloquent:

> Ixion fell in love with Hera and tried to rape her; when Hera told Zeus about it, Zeus wished to determine whether what she said was true. So he fashioned a cloud in the image of Hera and laid it by the side of Ixion. When Ixion boasted that he had lain

---

[210] Dia is the other name of Hebe, the daughter of Hera. It is often associated with Hera herself, probably because of its etymology (Dia: the one who belongs to Zeus). Cf. Kerenyi (1951) 150. If so, it is another clue to Ixion's erotic association with Hera.

[211] Apollodorus, Library, Epitome 1.20.Diodorus (Library 4.69.1) suggests that Centaurus was fathered by Apollo and Stilbe, daughter of the Thessalian river Peneus flowing from mount Pindus.

[212] Pindar, Pythian 2. 44ff.

[213] Pindar, Pythian 2. 48.

[214] 'If only you would bear in mind the fate of Ixion, you would never have dreamed of falling in love with beings so much above you. For he, you remember is bent and stretched across the heaven like a wheel.' Philostratus, Life of Apollonius of Tyana 6.40. Kereyni (1951) 160, says that later this fiery wheel was brought in Tartarus. There, he was spinning eternally. Only when Orpheus came to bring back his wife Eurydice did the wheel stop for a while, thanks to the charming music of the singer's lyre.

with Hera, Zeus punished him by tying him on a wheel, on which he was turned around by winds up in the air.[215]

Centaurs inherited the savage nature of Ixion. After Ixion's condemnation, his son Peirithoos (or Peirithous) became king of the Lapiths. Since Ixion was their grandfather, the Centaurs claimed a share in the rule. 'This first dispute, however, was settled peaceably and the Centaurs were given Mount Pelion as their territory'.[216] Trouble began when Peirithoos married a princess called Hippodameia. The centaurs were invited to the wedding, since they were related. For a while the wedding-party went on without trouble, but soon it became obvious that the centaurs could not handle their wine. They became very drunk and their lustful nature, just like that of Ixion, drove them to fall upon the Lapith women. One of the centaurs, Eurytion, even attempted to carry off the bride. One of the most savage battles in the history of Greek myths broke out, so popular that artists depicted it on vases and on the Parthenon sculptures in the 5th c. B.C.[217] Most of the vivid descriptions of this battle come from Apollodorus' *Library* (2.5.4 and *Epitome* 1.20.2) from Plutarch's *Life of Theseus* and the most vivid *Metamorphoses* of Ovid (book 12), which preserves some fifty names of centaurs.

Both the Lapiths and the centaurs suffered great losses. One of the Lapiths, Caeneus, was endowed with an invulnerable body, a gift of Poseidon. He was formerly a woman, Caenis, son of Elatus,[218] so beautiful that she rejected all suitors. Poseidon lusted after her and one day he came out of the sea and raped her. As a reward, he offered her the grant of any wish. She asked the god to turn her into an invulnerable man, so that she would suffer no such endurance in the future. Poseidon granted her the wish, adding that she/he would never die by sword.[219] He was brave and killed five centaurs, Antimachus, Styphelus, Bromus, Elymus and Pyracmus with his axe.[220] During the battle against the Lapiths, the centaurs realized his power and since they could not kill him otherwise, they surrounded

---

[215] Apollodorus, Library, Epitome 1, 20 (transl. Syropoulos).
[216] March (2014) 116.
[217] The battle was also depicted on the western frieze of the temple of Zeus at Olympia and the western pediment of the temple of Apollo at Bassae. Pausanias describes how the battles of Hercules with the centaurs were represented on the throne of Apollo at Amyclae, near Sparta. Pausanias, Description of Greece 3.18.10. Quintus Smyrnaeus says that the same theme was found on the shield of Eurypylus, grandson of Hercules (Quintus Smyrnaeus, Fall of Troy 6.274ff).
[218] Ovid, Metamorphoses 12. 189ff.
[219] Hesiod, Catalogue of Women 87 M-W; Apollonius, Argonautica 1.57-64; Apollodorus, Epitome 1.22; Virgil, Aeneid 6.448-9.
[220] Ovid, Metamorphoses 12.459.

and struck him with fir-trees or oaks, so many that the mounts Orthrys and Pelion were stripped bare of trees;[221] they hammered him deep under the ground.[222] Then he underwent yet another transformation, since from the middle of the pile of trees that weighed above him, a bird with golden wings flew up in the air.[223]

Finally, the centaurs were subdued, especially with the help of the great Athenian hero Theseus who was invited to the wedding, since Peirithoos was his best friend. According to Ovid's *Metamorphoses*, the centaur Petraeus was trying to uproot an oak tree, when Peirithoos hurled a spear and pinned his body on that oak tree. Then Peirithoos killed Lycus and Chromis, Helops and Dictys. Dictys was trying to escape when he fell down a cliff, onto the top of a huge ash-tree, which impaled his dying body on its broken spikes. Theseus killed many of the monsters. In the following passage by Ovid, Nestor describes the fight:

> *I saw [the centaur] Petraeus trying to uproot an acorn-laden oak and as his arms embraced it and he forced it to and fro, rocking its tottering trunk, Pirithous, hurling a lance that pierced Petraeus' ribs, pinned fast his writhing chest to the tough wood. The prowess of Pirithous, men say, laid [the centaur] Lycus low, laid [the centaur] Chromis low, but each gave less distinction to the victor than [the centaurs] Dictys and Helops. Helops was transfixed by a lance that struck his forehead from the right and pierced to his left ear. Dictys, in flight before the onslaught of Ixion's son [Peirithous], slipped on a mountain precipice and fell headlong; his weight broke a huge mountain-ash whose splintered spike impaled him in his groin.*
>
> *For vengeance [the centaur] Aphareus was there and tried to throw a rock wrenched from the mountainside. But Aegides [Theseus] caught him as he threw and smashed his giant elbow with a club of oak. Enough! No time nor wish to do to death that good-for-nothing! On [centaur] Bienor's back he leapt (a back not used to carry a soul except himself) and, knees gripping his flanks and left hand holding fast his head of hair, he swung the knotted club and smashed his mouth, screaming out threats, and broke his bony brow. That club then felled [the centaurs] Nedymnus and Lycopes, famed for his javelin, and [centaur] Hippasos whose long beard draped his chest, and Ripheus too whose stature overtopped the forest trees, and [centaur] Thereus who would capture mountain bears of Haemonia [Thessalia] and bring them home alive and snarling.*
>
> *Theseus' triumphs in the fight were too much for [centaur] Demeleon. He tried with a huge heave to uproot an ancient pine, a sturdy trunk, and, when his efforts*

---

[221] Ovid, Metamorphoses 12.494-522.
[222] Pindar, Fragment 166: 'Caeneus, struck by the green fir-trees, cleft the ground with his foot, where he stood, and passed beneath the earth'.
[223] Ovid, Metamorphoses 12.494-522.

failed, he snapped it off and threw it at his foe. But as the missile came Theseus drew back beyond its range, on Pallas's [Athene's] advice (or so he'd have us think). But still the trunk did not fall idle: from tall Crantor's neck it severed his left shoulder and his breast. Crantor, Achilles, was your father's squire; Amyntor, leader of the Dolopes, worsted in war, had sent him as a gift, to be a pledge of peace and loyalty.

When Aeacides [Peleus], at a distance, saw the lad cleft by that hideous wound, 'Crantor,' he cried, 'my favorite, at least receive from me your death-right fight!' And with his powerful arm and all his passion's strength he hurled his spear full at [the centaur] Demeleon. It broke his ribs and hung there quivering in the box of bones. The centaur wrenched the shaft away without the point (the shaft would hardly come); the point stuck in his lung. His very agony gave him wild strength. Despite the wound he reared and pounded Peleus with his horse's hooves. On helm and ringing shield Peleus received the lashing hooves and, so defended, held his lance-point levelled and with one thrust pierced the centaur's shoulder and his two-formed chest. Already at a longer range he'd slain [the centaurs] Phlegraeos and Hyles and, hand-to-hand, Iphinous and Clanis; now to them he added [the centaur] Dorylas who wore a cap of wolf-skin on his head with, for a lance, a splendid pair of bull's horns red with blood.[224]

The centaurs who escaped fled to Peloponnese. Here, they were to experience more savage battles with the Peloponnesian hero, Hercules. As is the case of the troubles in Thessaly, everything started with an act of *xenia*, offer of hospitality, gone wrong.

Hercules was after the wild boar of Erymanthus, when he stopped at the cave of the centaur Pholus, on Mount Pholoe. Unlike the rest of the centaurs, he was not fathered by Ixion, but by a satyr named Silenus and a nymph.[225] Once more, the account of Apollodorus is very vivid: Hercules was offered hospitality by Pholus in his cave. The menu was simple: cooked meat for the hero and raw meat for the monstrous creature. But Hercules was notorious – and for this loved by comic writers in the classical period – for his huge appetite for food and drink. He asked for wine which seems like a harmless enough offering, especially since hospitality demands that one take care of one's guest. But Pholus was the wine-keeper of all centaurs, who shared a common jar of wine. He was afraid to open it, lest the rest of the centaurs got offended, since they had agreed to drink commonly, at the same time. Hercules insisted and Pholus gave in. The smell of sweet wine travelled amongst the leaves of the forest and soon a horde of angry centaurs gathered

---

[224] Ovid, Metamorphoses 12, 341-282 (transl. Melvile).
[225] Apollodorus 2.5.4; Diodorus, Library 4.12.3-8; Pausanias, Description of Greece 3.18.10.

outside the cave, armed with rocks and fir-trees.[226] Hercules repelled the first two, Achius and Agrius and chased the rest up to Malea, where they took refuge with another kind of Centaur, Cheiron.[227] Hercules chased them and shot many of them dead. The rest were taken in at Eleusis by Poseidon who hid them away on a mountain. Cheiron died accidentally by an arrow that went through another centaur and struck him on the knee. 'As for Pholus, as he was pulling an arrow out of a corpse, he marveled that such a little object could destroy such enormous adversaries. Just then it slipped from his hand, fell on his foot and instantly killed him. When Herakles returned to Pholus, he found Pholus dead, so he buried him and proceeded on to find the boar'.[228]

Accordingly we are presented with two centaurs of a different nature, compared to the rest: Pholus and Cheiron. The first stands out for his sense of hospitality – a most sacred value of human civilization; the latter as a wise tutor of young heroes. It should be stressed, however, that these two centaurs also differ because of their parentage. Although most of the known centaurs were thought of as children of the cloud-Hera and Ixion,[229] Pholus and Cheiron have different origins.

As already mentioned, Pholus was the son of the satyr Silenus and a Melian nymph. The other one, Cheiron, was fathered by the primordial god Cronus and Philyra, one of Ocean's daughters. Cronus desired Philyra but he could not escape the vigilant gaze of his wife, Rhea. So he transformed himself into a horse and thus he mated with Philyra.[230] This is what is also told by Hyginus,[231] Ovid,[232] and by Eumelus of Corinth or Arctinus of Miletus in a lost poem entitled *Titanomachy*, fragment 6 (from Scholiast on Apollonius Rhodius 1. 554): 'The author of the *War of the Giants* (*Gigantomakhia*) says that Kronos (Cronus) took the shape of a horse and lay with Philyra, the daughter of Okeanos. Through this cause, Kheiron (Chiron) was born a kentauros (centaur): his wife was Khariklo (Chariclo)'. Apollonius Rhodius says that Cronus had taken Philyra to the homonymous island. When the two lovers were surprised by Hera, Cronus leapt out of bed and galloped off in the form of a long-maned stallion. Philyra came to the Pelasgian ridges and 'There

---

[226] Diodorus says that the jar had been left behind by Dionysus, the god of wine, with instructions to be opened only upon Hercules' arrival. When the smell of wine reached the rest of the Centaurs they got mad or drunk and attacked the cave. Diodorus, Library 4.12.3.
[227] Apollodorus, Library 2.83-87.
[228] Apollodorus, Library 2.83-87.
[229] Apollodorus, Library, Epitomy 1.20; Ovid, Metamorphoses 9.123, 12.210, 12.504; Diodorus, Library 4.12.6, 4.69.5, 4.70.1).
[230] Hyginus, Fabulae 138. According to Hyginus, after Philyra saw the monstrous child she had born, she asked Hera to change her form and she was turned into a linden.
[231] Hyginus, Fabulae 138.
[232] Ovid, Metamorphoses 6.126ff

she gave birth to the monstrous Kheiron (Chiron), half horse and half divine, the offspring of a lover in questionable shape'.[233] Their offspring was an immortal centaur, Cheiron – half-brother of Zeus. Just like the hospitable Pholus, he stands out because of his wisdom and kindness. He was very skilled in various arts, such as medicine,[234] archery, music, hunting and poetry,[235] and so he became a popular tutor of many eponymous heroes, who were educated by him in his cave.[236] Achilles,[237] Jason,[238] Asclepius, Aristaeus and the hunter Actaeon were amongst his pupils. Ptolemy Hephaestion presents him as a tutor to gods, such as Dionysus, to whom Cheiron taught chants, dances, the rites and initiations.[239] Hyginus informs us that 'he surpassed not only all the other centaurs, but also men in justice'.[240]

Like all other centaurs, Cheiron lived on Mount Pelion, but he was driven away along with the rest by the Lapiths. Despite his beastly form he was not deprived of love and he fathered many children before willingly choosing to forfeit his immortality and die, due to his suffering a painful wound. Chariclo bore to him the Pelionid nymphs,[241] the demi-god Carystus, who lived on the island of Euboea and gave his name to the homonymous city of south Euboea,[242] and the prophetess Ocyrrhoe, who was turned into a mare by Zeus for revealing too many secrets to mortals.[243] Endeis, mother of Peleus and Telamon, was also thought to be his daughter (thus she is the grandmother of Achilles),[244] although Plutarch and Pausanias name Skeiron, and not Cheiron, as her father.[245] Cheiron was the one who helped Peleus win over the sea-nymph Thetis and gave him a strong spear to pass on to his unborn son, Achilles.[246] His prophetic powers helped the Argonauts

---

[233] Apollonius Rhodius 2.1231; Hyginus, Fabulae 138, Astronomica 2.38; Ovid, Metamorphoses 6.126, 7.352; Pliny the Elder, Natural History 7.197.
[234] Aelian says that Achilles learned the art of healing by Cheiron. Aelian, On Animals 2.18. Cf. Homer, Iliad 11.832.
[235] Homer, Iliad 11.831.
[236] His skills on music, hunting, archery and prophecy came from Apollo and Artemis. Cf. Xenophon, Cynegeticus 1; Pindar, Pythian 9. 65.
[237] Homer says that Peleus, the father of Achilles, was related to Cheiron (Iliad16.143, 19.390).
[238] Hesiod, Theogony 993ff, Catalogue of Women, fragment 13; Pindar, Pythian Ode 4.101ff, Nemean Ode 3. 53ff; Apollonius Rhodius, Argonautica 1.32.
[239] Ptolemy Hephaestion, New History 4 (from Photius' Myriobiblon 190).
[240] Hyginus, Astronomica 2.38ff.
[241] Pindar, Pythian 5.
[242] Scholiast on Pindar's Pythian 4.181; Eustathius, Ad Homerum 281.
[243] Ovid, Metamorphoses 2.635.
[244] Hyginus, Fabulae 41.
[245] Plutarch, Theseus 10.3; Pausanias, Description of Greece 2.29.9.
[246] Homer, Iliad 19.390ff; Pindar, Nemean 3.52, Isthmian 8.38ff; Alcaeus, Fragment 42; Quintus

when they met him on their way to Colchis, since many of them had been his pupils.[247] He had also foretold to Apollo, when he saw Cyrene wrestling a lion, that he would carry her off to Libya and make her a founder of a great line.[248]

His kindness is exhibited in another odd story. When the hunter Actaeon was turned into a deer by Artemis, because he had accidentally seen her bathing naked, his fifty dogs attacked him and tore him to pieces. After that, they were anxiously howling and looking for their master to no avail. Searching for him they came to Cheiron's cave and the good centaur made an image of Actaeon so lifelike that the dogs were comforted.[249]

Since he was immortal, his end had to come from another extra-ordinary being: Hercules. The end of Cheiron is very similar to that of Pholus, and the influence of one story on the other is more than obvious. Apollodorus' account in the *Library* is very detailed. The hero was fighting the rest of lustful and savage centaurs on Mount Pholoe with fire-brands and arrows and chased them as far as Malea, where Cheiron had fled after being driven out of his native land by the Lapiths. Hercules shot an arrow at the centaur Elatus, but the missile pierced the arm of Elatus and struck the knee of Cheiron.[250] Others, say that Cheiron was simply curious of how such a tiny thing could kill such a big beast and he pulled out an arrow from the wound of a dead centaur to examine it. A tap with his fingertip on the poisonous tip of Hercules' arrows[251] meant instant death.[252]

Shocked and upset, Hercules pulled out the arrow, but it was too late, since his arrows were dipped in the poison of the Hydra of Lerna. However, Cheiron could not die though his suffering was unbearable. Ironically, the greatest of healers could not heal himself. Seeing this, Prometheus, released by Hercules from Caucasus, where he had been chained by Zeus,[253] proposed to Zeus to grant him the immortality of Cheiron – since obviously cosmic balance demands that this is something not lost – and Cheiron, relieved, accepted it, and so he died.[254] Pitying him, Zeus turned him into a constellation – the constellation of Sagittarius.[255]

Smyrnaeus, Fall of Troy 1.592ff; Valerius Flaccus, Argonautica 1.130ff; Statius, Achilleid 1.105ff, Silvae 1.2.215ff.
[247] Apollonius Rhodius, Argonautica 1.55.
[248] Apollonius Rhodius, Argonautica 2.512.
[249] Apollodorus, Library 3.30.
[250] Same detail in Diodorus, Library 4.12.8.
[251] Ovid, Metamorphoses, 2.649ff.
[252] Hyginus, Astronomica 2.38ff.
[253] Apollodorus, Library 1.119.
[254] Apollodorus, Library 2.83-87.
[255] Hyginus, Astronomica 2.38ff; Ovid, Fasti 5.379.

Finally, Hercules' encounter with another lustful, savage centaur is narrated in Sophocles' 5th c. B.C. tragedy *Trachiniae*, where there is a description of how the Thessalian Centaur Nessus fled his land after the Lapith wars and made himself a ferryman, carrying people across the river Euenus on his back for a fee.[256] When Hercules was on his way home with his bride-to-be Deianeira, Nessus offered to carry her across the flooded river. Half-way through he attempted to rape her, causing Hercules to shoot him with his arrows. Poisoned by the Hydra's blood, Nessus had enough strength to take his revenge. He advised Deianeira to collect his semen that had fallen on the ground with the blood that was flowing from his wound and mix them into a potion that would win back Hercules' love, if he ever proved unfaithful to her.[257] When Hercules returned home with young Iole after an expedition, Deianeira, in fear of losing his love, but not jealous of Iole, smeared his robe with the elixir, unwittingly causing Hercules to die in pain.[258]

Very popular in art, Centaurs are prominent on the metopes of the Parthenon on the Acropolis of Athens.[259] They are found on the metopes of the south wall and they are part of the scenes that depict the famous Centauromachy, the battle of the Lapiths against the Centaurs, in which Theseus took part as a king of Athens. Some of the Centaurs are wearing animal skins and some hold tree branches as weapons. The surviving metopes seem to convey a picture of the Centaurs' supremacy over the Lapiths, but we are not sure about the stage of battle presented here. They appear next to the metopes of the exploits of Theseus against the Amazons. Both the Amazons and the Centaurs seem to symbolize disorder and the unnatural. The Athenians' superiority over them could well represent the triumph of reason and order over animal passion and chaos.[260] The Parthenon, built after the supremacy of Greeks over the Persians, became the ultimate symbol of the reinstitution of order. It also became a reminder of the leading role of the Athenians.

---

[256] Apollodorus, Library 2.151ff.
[257] Apollodorus, Library 2.151ff; Diodorus, Library 4.36.3, adds olive oil and wine to the elixir of semen and blood.
[258] For the unintentional murder of Hercules by his wife, see Sohocles' Trachiniae ('Women of Trachis').
[259] The metopes are a series of 92 panels which decorate the frieze of the Parthenon on the outside walls. They are part of the complex and elaborate depiction of mythological and historical traditions and together with the pediments, Ionic frieze and Doric frieze of the Parthenon constitute the impressive decoration of the monument. 15 of these metopes, mostly from the south wall, are currently at the British Museum, in the Parthenon marbles section. Many of them, especially the central ones, were destroyed in 1687 by a Venetian cannonball, during an attack on Athens.
[260] Stockstad & Cothren (2011) 133.

Since the Athenians, represented by their king Theseus, had saved the Greeks in the once-upon-a-time mythological past, they had the right to remind everyone of their prominent role as generals of the Greeks during the victorious Persian Wars.

'Both Centaurs and Amazons symbolize the Persians, through a system of polarizing contrasts and proportions. The Persians, like the mythical creatures the Athenians see in the metopes of the Parthenon, offended the rules of trade, i.e. give and take, which govern a civilized society. They demanded earth and water from the Greeks, without respecting the limits of the dispute. They are presented as asymmetrical, unbalanced societies, either hyper-masculine, as that of the centaurs, or hyper-feminine, as that of the Amazons. Both of these societies are problematic, uncivilized, immediately seductive and threatening, a threat to human institutions and to human community in general. The specific characteristics of the Persians are very similar to those of the Amazons and centaurs. Presented as catalysts of all civilized modes of behavior, they should be excluded from all relationships of reciprocity. The analogy between the centaurs, Amazons and Persians is the most obvious and the most historically accurate of all analogies that were repeated in depictions of these legendary battles in the art of the 5th century'.[261]

Echidna (Εχιδνα)

There is a certain mesmerizing, lethal charm in snakes. The calm, rhythmic uncoiling of their lean bodies can be seductive and dangerous. 'Just like a woman' to the view of ancient Greek males. The combination of serpentine and female qualities finds its culmination in the form of Echidna. Half-woman and half snake, she was a menace to men, who could not resist her attraction.

Her parentage is complicated. Apollodorus informs us that she was a daughter of the dark Tartarus (the name also stands for the darkest depths of the underworld) and Gaea, the Earth.[262] Hesiod, in his *Theogony* suggests Phorcys and Ceto, the monstrous sea-gods as her parents.[263] Later, Pausanias imagined even more fierce parents for Echidna: the mythical son of Argus, Peiras or Peirasus and Styx, the river that flows in the underworld.[264]

---

[261] From a public lecture by S. Syropoulos, Amazons and Propaganda. Myth as a political tool in Classical Athens, Rhodes, 5 November 2013.
[262] Apollodorus, Library 2. 1-4.
[263] Hesiod, Theogony 2.95.
[264] Pausanias, Description of Greece, 8.18.1.

According to Hesiod, she is a fearsome, immortal maiden who lives in the land of the Arimaspians,[265] underground. She is associated with Typhon, and since he was the one who challenged Zeus' supremacy and stands for all evil, she bore from him some of the most notorious monsters of Greek mythology: the terrible dog Orthus, Cerberus, the Hydra of Lerna and the abominable Chimaera:[266]

> *[And then Ceto:] in a beautiful cave bore another invincible monster*   296
> *resembling neither mortal men nor immortal gods,*
> *the divine Echidna with the cruel heart,*
> *half of whom was a maiden with sparkling eyes and beautiful cheeks,*
> *and the other half a huge snake terrible and gigantic,*   300
> *dappled and flesh-eating, deep in the depths of the holy ground.*
> *There lies her cave, under the hollow of a rock*
> *away from the immortal gods and the mortal men.*
> *There have the gods decided for her to have her famous lair.*
> *This is where she remained in the land of the Arimoi, under the earth,*
> *the abominable Echidna,*   305
> *the immortal maiden who never grows old.*
> *It is said that the she mingled erotically with Typhon, the fearsome, lawless, terrible one, she the playful-eyed maiden,*
> *and after she became pregnant she gave birth to cruel-hearted children.*
> *First she gave birth to Orthus, the dog of Geryon.*   310
> *Second she bore the invincible, the unspoken*
> *Cerberus, the flesh-eater, the bronze-voiced dog of Hades,*
> *the fifty-headed, merciless and strong.*
> *Third she gave birth to the Hydra of Lerna, whose mind was evil*
> *and who was nurtured by Hera of the white arms*   315
> *with relentless rage for powerful Hercules.*
> *And she was killed by the merciless sword of the son of Zeus,*
> *son of Amphitryon, with the warlike Iolaus,*
> *Hercules, with the will of Athena who shares spoils.*[267]

Quintus Smyrnaeus also confirms the parentage of Orthus and Cerberus by Echidna and Typhon.[268] Ovid agrees about the parentage of Cerberus and Hydra by Echidna and

---

[265] See chapter 1.
[266] Hesiod, Theogony 306.
[267] Hesiod, Theogony, 296-319 (transl. Syropoulos).
[268] Quintus Smyrnaeus, Fall of Troy, 6.249, 6.260.

Typhon,[269] and in one of the fragments of Bacchylides we read about the parentage of Cerberus.[270] The same is found in the Homeric Hymn 3.356 about the Chimaera. Apollodorus names a great number of monsters as her children by Typhon: Orthus, Chimaera, Ladon, the Dragon that guarded the apple-tree of the Hesperides, the Eagle of Zeus that ate the liver of Prometheus, the Sphinx and the sow of Crommyon, by the name Phaea, later killed by Theseus.[271] Finally, Nonnus, in his *Dionysiaca* mentions some serpentine son of Echidna, who was two-shaped (probably half man and half-snake), and spat poison just like his mother. He was killed by Ares.[272]

In his *Alexandra*, Lycophron suggested that Echidna did not live in the land of the Arimaspians but in the waters of the lake of Cilicia.[273] In his *Histories* Herodotus describes an encounter of Hercules with a monster which is half-woman and half-serpent, which could be identified with Echidna. According to this version, Hercules was passing through the land of Scythia, driving the cattle of Geryon back to Mycenae. As he came to a woodland area named Hylaien, he found a cave with a creature half-woman and half-serpent. He asked her if she knew where his mares, yoked to his chariot, had strayed. She offered to help him only if he would have intercourse with her. Hercules did so, hoping to find his animals, but the monster would not tell him, in the hope of keeping him with her for a longer time. Finally she gave the animals to Hercules, announcing that she was pregnant by him and asking him what she should do with his sons. Hercules set a test for their strength: he left a bow and a belt behind: the son that would be able to bent the hero's bow should stay in the land and the others should be cast out as exiles. Three boys were born, Agathyrsos, Gelonos and Scythes. Only Scythes managed to fulfill the task set by the father, Hercules. He remained at the land and became the forefather of the Scythians.[274] Whether this half-maiden, half-serpent monster is the Echidna of previous myths is not clear, but the description fits the account of Hesiod and Apollodorus.

Such a terrible monster could not have been subdued by ordinary men or heroes. Only a god or another monster could destroy her. One tradition confuses Echidna with the woman-headed serpent that dueled at Delphi and was killed by Apollo.[275] The description of the female snake (drakaina) that destroyed men and

---

[269] Ovid, Metamorphoses, 7.412, 9. 69.
[270] Bacchylides, Fragment 5. Orthus and Cerberus are mentioned as children of Echidna also by Quintus Smyrnaeus, Fall of Troy 6.240, 6.260.
[271] Apollodorus, Library 2.106, 2.32, 2.113, 2.120 3.52, Epitome 1. The parentage of the Eagle is attested also at Hyginus, Astronomica i2.15.
[272] Nonnus, Dionysiaca, 18.274.
[273] Lycophron, Alexandra 1351ff.
[274] Herodotus, Histories 4.9.1ff. A similar monster found in the Scythian land is also described by Valerius Flaccus (Argonautica 6.48ff).
[275] See chapter 2, Python.

sheep and was nurtured by Hera to plague men, is found in the Homeric Hymns.[276] This is the Echidna/Drakaina that was killed by Apollo.

The most widely accepted version has the monstrous Argus killing her while she was asleep. Argus was named Panoptes, the all-seeing.[277] He gained this epithet for the number of eyes that covered his body.[278] Some say that he had four eyes,[279] others say that he had a hundred. Half of them remained vigilant while the other half were asleep. According to Apollodorus, Argus was the son of Agenor, grandson of Ecbasus, fathered by Argus (fathered by Zeus and Niobe). Since he claimed he was from the line of Zeus, he possessed superhuman strength. He killed a bull that raged through Arcadia and used his hide as a cloak. He also killed a Satyr who stole the herds of the Arcadians. He avenged the murder of Apis by slaying the guilty, Thelxion and Telchis, and finally, he waited until Echidna was asleep and killed her. Argus was killed with a stone by Hermes, who thus earned the epithet Argeiphontes, the *Argos-slayer*.[280]

It is obvious that in both these cases Echidna is not immortal, as Hesiod depicted her.

Scylla (Σκύλλα)

Scylla enters world literature in Homer's *Odyssey*. In book 12 of the epic, Odysseus receives sea-faring advice from the witch Circe. Just like Calypso, or Nausicaa, Circe was not able to resist the charm of the hero and she gives him instructions on how to avoid dangers during his return journey to Ithaca. Many other monsters were bred by Amphitrite, the wife of Poseidon; but there are monsters which feast on monsters. Such is the terrible Scylla. Like the sirens, her voice sounds harmless, like that of a puppy, but she is so terrible that not even gods can face her without a shiver. Her appearance is most weird. Six necks with terrible heads equipped with triple rows of teeth and twelve feet that seem to dangle useless in the air. Her body is concealed in a cave, and we must assume that the necks are so long that she can prolong them like serpents do, and she snatches unsuspecting sailors from the decks of their ships, as well as dolphins, sharks and other sea-monsters. The proverbial phrase, *between Scylla and Charybdis* means a situation that is nearly

---

[276] Cf. Homeric Hymn 3, to Apollo, 356ff
[277] For Argus Panoptes, see Hesiod or Cercops of Miletus, The Aegimius (Greek epic 7th c. B.C.); Aeschylus, Suppliant Women 303-5, Prometheus Bound 566-74; Euripides, Suppliant Women 1113-18; Apollodorus, Library 2.1.2-3; Ovid, Metamorphoses 1.622-723; Pliny, Natural History 16.239.
[278] Apollodorus, Library 2.4ff.
[279] Hesiod or Cercops of Miletus, Aegimius, Fragment 5 (from Scholiast on Homer's Iliad 2.24).
[280] Apollodorus, Library 2.4.ff.

impossible. Scylla is the lesser of two evils. Directly opposite Scylla is Charybdis, another terrible monster, who utilizes a kind of monstrous whirlpool, sucking into its bottomless depths the ships that are caught in its vortices.

> In that cavern Skylla lives, whose howling is terror.   85
> Her voice indeed is only as loud as a new-born puppy
> could make, but she herself is an evil monster. No one,
> not even a god encountering her, could be glad at that sight.
> She has twelve feet, and all of them wave in the air. She has six
> necks upon her, grown to great length, and upon each neck   90
> there is a horrible head, with teeth in it, set in three rows
> close together and stiff, full of black death. Her body
> from the waist down is holed up inside the hollow cavern,
> but she holds her heads poked out and away from the terrible hollow,
> and there she fishes, peering all over the cliffside, looking   95
> for dolphins or dogfish to catch or anything bigger,
> some sea monster, of whom Amphitrite keeps so many;
> never can sailors boast aloud that their ship has passed her
> without any loss of men, for with each of her heads she snatches
> one man away and carries him off from the dark-prowed vessel.   100
> 'The other cliff is lower; you will see it, Odysseus,
> for they lie close together, you could even cast with an arrow
> across. There is a great fig tree that grows there, dense with foliage,
> and under this shining Charybdis sucks down the black water.
> For three times a day she flows it up, and three times she sucks it   105
> terribly down; may you not be there when she sucks down water,
> for not even the Earthshaker could rescue you out of that evil.
> but sailing your ship swiftly drive her past and avoid her,
> and make for Skylla's rock instead, since it is far better
> to mourn six friends lost out of your ship than the whole company'.[281]

So Circe advises Odysseus to sacrifice six of his companions rather than to see all of them lost in Charybdis. A captain's choice is hard. But Odysseus goes with the advice of the witch. He does not tell anything about Scylla to his shipmates and tries to steer clear of Charybdis. He does not mean to go without a fight. As he commands his men to stay away from Charybdis, he arms himself with weapons to face the monster:

---

[281] Homer, Odyssey 12. 85-110.

PARTLY HUMAN 75

Scylla as a maiden with a kētos tail and dog heads sprouting from her body. Detail from a red-figure bell-crater in the Louvre, 450–425 BCE. This form of Scylla was prevalent in ancient depictions, though very different from the description in Homer, where she is land-based and more dragon-like

> *We in fear of destruction kept our eyes on Charybdis,*
> *but meanwhile Skylla out of the hollow vessel snatched six*   245
> *of my companions, the best of them for strength and hands' work,*
> *and when I turned to look at the ship, with my other companions*
> *I saw their feet and hands from below, already lifted*
> *high above me, and they cried out to me and called me*
> *by name, the last time they ever did it, heart's sorrow.*   250
> *And as a fisherman with a very long rod, on a jutting*
> *rock, will cast his treacherous bait for the little fishes,*
> *and sinks the horn of a field-raging ox into the water,*
> *then hauls them up and throws them on the dry land, gasping*

> *and struggling, so they gasped and struggled as they were hoisted   255*
> *up the cliff. Right in her doorway she ate them up. They were screaming*
> *and reaching out their hands to me in this horrid encounter.*
> *That was the most pitiful scene that these eyes have looked on*
> *In my sufferings as I explored the routes of water.*[282]

A most interesting fact is pointed out by Mercedes Aguirre Castro in her very informative article 'Scylla: Hideous monster or femme fatale? A case of contradiction between literary and artistic evidence'. Aguirre Castro showed that the iconographical representation of Scylla, especially during the 6th and 5th c. B.C., does not accord with the literary descriptions, such as Homer's description above. 'The earliest representation of her would seem to be the image of an Etruscan ivory box with reliefs dated about 600 B.C. On the box there appears a monster like an octopus or giant squid next to a ship; and besides the Scylla image there is a scene with the Cyclops'.[283] The author describes the evolution of Scylla's iconographical appearances up to the second c. B.C. and she concludes that more than appearances, it was the character of Scylla that made her a monster.

In the most recent work about Scylla, Marianne Hopman points out that 'although (the) Odyssey provides us with our earliest extant source for both Scylla and Odysseus' encounter with her, it is very likely that the Scylla narrative, like Circe, the Cyclops and other episodes of the apologoi, draws on traditional material that is reshaped to accommodate the specific interests of the *Odyssey.*'[284] By the 5th c. B.C., Scylla stood out as a measure of monstrosity. Only terrible females can be compared to her, such as Clytemnestra, who killed her husband Agamemnon after his return from Troy, to avenge the death of their daughter, Iphigeneia, at the hands of her father: 'Such boldness has she, a woman, to slay a man. What hideous monster could I call her befittingly? An Amphisbaina, or a Scylla, tenanting the rocks, a menace to mariners, a raging mother of Hades, breathing relentless war against her husband'.[285] Aguirre Castro suggests that Scylla's monstrosity is comparable to the character of the 'femmes fatales, like Circe or Calypso, who, in spite of their beautiful and seductive appearance, hide something sinister or terrible'. [286]

The transcendental form of this monster had fascinated writers since early antiquity and until the days of Plato (4th c. B.C.). In his *Republic* he uses her as

---

[282] Homer, Odyssey 12. 243-59.
[283] Aguirre Castro (2002) 321 and n. 11.
[284] Hopman (2013) 24.
[285] Aescylus, Agamemnon 1232ff (transl. Syropoulos).
[286] Aguirre Castro (2002) 328.

one of the monsters *par excellence,* when it comes to confusing forms: 'one of these natures that the ancient fables tell of, as that of the Chimaera, or Scylla, or Cerberus, and the numerous other examples that are told of many forms grown together in one'.[287]

Monstrosity, however, can be more complex than what first meets the eye; especially when it comes to origins. The story of Scylla could be not a story about the magic of love, but about love and magic. At least this is how later poets, like Ovid (1st c. B.C.-1st c. A.D.) imagined it. In his *Metamorphoses* he claims that according to old poets, Scylla was once a beautiful girl. She was so attractive, that many suitors were after her, but she rejected them all and preferred the company of *Nymphae Pelagi,* Sea-Nymphs. She was out there with the nymphs, one day, talking to her friend Galatea, hearing how she was also amorously wooed by Cyclops. The girls' chat was over and Scylla got undressed to swim in a protected little cove. 'Suddenly, breaking the waves of the sea, Glaucus appeared'.[288]

Glaucus was once a mortal from the city of Anthedon in Boeotia. He was a keen fisherman and loved the sea. One day he caught some fish and threw them onto some plant, only to see the fish eat it, come back to life and wriggle their way back to the sea. Glaucus could not resist his curiosity. He ate the plant, too. As a result he grew a green beard, tail and fins of a fish, and long hair that covered his back. He plunged into the sea and the gods of the sea made him immortal.[289]

Now, mesmerized by the beauty of naked Scylla, Glaucus expressed his love for her, but his looks were so strange that she could not decide whether he was a god or a monster. She fled in terror and Glaucus, overwhelmed by the realization of his repulsiveness, hasted for the magic halls of Circe. If magic was what turned him into what he had been, perhaps magic could give him what he desired most: Scylla.

But love stories are complicated. Circe, the witch, was bewitched by Glaucus. She expressed her love for him but his response was not what she had hoped for. 'Sooner shall green leaves grow in the sea or seaweed on the hills, than I shall change my love while Scylla lives'.[290] Rage filled the heart of the goddess Circe, but she directed it to Scylla, not Glaucus. Sorcery comes in handy, when one wants to take revenge. Circe used her ill-famed herbs to create a terrible potion, which she poured into the still waters of the quiet little bay, where Scylla used to bathe, whispering a round of magic incantations nine times. When Scylla came into the

---

[287] Plato, Republic 588 c.
[288] Ovid, Metamorphoses 13.729ff.
[289] Apollonius, Argonautica 1.1310-28; Pausanias 9.22.6-7; Atheneaeus 7.296-97c; Ovid Metamorphoses 13. 898-14.69.
[290] Ovid, Metamorphoses 13. 729ff.

water and she was waist-deep in it, she saw her feet turning into gaping jaws of barking beasts, like the vile hound of the Underworld.

Instead of rushing into Circe's embrace, Glaucus fled terrified and heartbroken. Scylla stayed there, where she was, and became the monster that would deprive Odysseus of six of his comrades. She would have sunk the Trojan fleet of Aeneas too, but before they arrived she was transformed into a reef whose rocks rise up to this day, and sailors avoid it by steering away from it.[291]

As time passes by, the appearance of Scylla changes, at least in the works of Latin poets. According to Virgil (1st c. B.C.), Aeneas, the Trojan hero who was to become the forefather of the Romans, had to pass through Scylla and Charybdis, just like Odysseus.

The transformation of Scylla from a beautiful girl into a monster is not Ovid's innovation. It is also found in Nonnus' *Dionysiaca* (5th c. B.C.), only this time it is the god of the sea who has the power to turn a beautiful girl into a dangerous rocky cliff: '[Poseidon] slept with Scylla and turned her into a cliff in the water'.[292] According to a much later source, the Byzantine poet and grammarian John Tzetzes (c. 111—1180 A.D.), Scylla was loved by Poseidon and she was turned into a monster by the jealous queen of Poseidon, Amphitrite.[293] Tzetzes informs us that Scylla was a daughter of Nisus of Megara.[294] Today she is the cape Rhegion in Sicily, protruding into the rough sea, a dangerous place for the sailors who pass by it.[295]

A few centuries later, Virgil (1st c. B.C.) claimed that Scylla became one of the monsters that guard the doors of Hades (the others are the Centaurs, Briareus, Lerna, Chimaera, the Gorgons, the Harpies and the three-bodied Geryon).[296] The same opinion is shared by the 1st c. B.C. Roman poet Statius.[297]

Sphinx (Σφιγξ)

The Sphinx was in all probability imported from Egypt, after the Greeks had come into contact with Egyptian civilization. Nowadays we know that the Greeks had

---

[291] The story is found in Ovid, Metamorphoses 13. 7230-14.74. For some people, this location lies between Sicily and the southern part of Italy.
[292] Nonnus, Dionysiaca 42.409ff.
[293] Scholia by Tzetzes on Alexandra or Cassandra of Lycophron 650 (Müller, 1811, p.340). Cf. Servius on Aeneid 3.420.
[294] Müller (1811) 716. The same paternity is recorded by Ovid, Fasti 4.499.
[295] Müller (1811) 341. Cf. Seneca, Hercules Furens 375ff: 'Sooner shall... Scylla join the Sicilian and Ausonian shores' [i.e. the phrase that means it will never happen].
[296] Virgil, Aeneid 6.287ff.
[297] Statius, Thebaid 4.536ff; Silvae 5.3.260ff.

trade relations with the Egyptians as early as the 1500s B.C.²⁹⁸ During the Bronze Age, Greece had established extended relations with the Egyptians. The figure of the Sphinx was already a trademark of Egypt.²⁹⁹ The Greeks had already come up with names for the strange statues of these creatures; Herodotus had categorized them into Hiercaoshpinxes (griffin-like creatures with the head of a hawk, *hierax* in Greek) and Criosphinxes (ram-headed Sphinxes, from *Crios*, ram in Greek). Various interpretations relate the name to the Greek verb *sphingo* (σφίγγω), meaning to squeeze or strangle, probably inspired by the lion body of the Sphinx, which strangles its prey by biting its throat and holding it down until it suffocates to death. A different theory comes from the historian Susan Bauer who suggested that the Greek term was a corruption of the Egyptian term *shesepankh*, which means living

Marble Sphinx, dated 540 BCE, in the Acropolis Museum, Athens

---

²⁹⁸ This is attested by a drawing at the tomb of a high officer named Senmud at Thebes of Egypt, which clearly depicts Minoans bearing goods. The date of the drawing is around 1500 B.C.
²⁹⁹ Regier (2004) 54, 59,177.

image and most probably referred to the statue of the Sphinx, carved out of *living rock*, found at the location of the construction, not brought from another place.[300]

In any case there are two notable differences between the Egyptian and the Greek Sphinx. The Egyptian monster is a creature with the body of a lion and the head of a man.[301] The Egyptian Sphinx is a benevolent creature, associated with the safe-guarding of tombs and the passage of souls to the afterlife. When the creature is imported into Greece, it undergoes notable changes. First of all, it becomes female. And it becomes malevolent. The Greeks could obviously not tolerate good will in a creature whose form is so monstrous.

Hesiod knows of a Sphinx fathered by the terrible dog Orthrus and Echidna, but he calls her Phix (Φιξ), not Sphinx.[302] She is definitely the monster that plagued the city of Oedipus, since this is clearly stated in line 326.[303] She was born in the land of the Arimoi. Apollodorus calls her a daughter of Typhon and Echidna.[304] Others claim that she was an offspring of Typhon and Chimaera.[305] In any case she becomes mostly known through her association with one of the most cursed families in Greek myths, the family of Laius.[306] Very popular in art, she is mostly depicted as a monster with the head of a woman and wings. In the old *Dictionary of Greek and Roman Biography, Mythology and Geography* it is suggested that although the legend of the Sphinx appears to have come from Egypt, the Greek Sphinx is depicted in a different manner. 'The Egyptian Sphinx is the figure of a lion without wings in a lying attitude, the upper part of the body being that of a human being. The Sphinxes appear in Egypt to have been set up in avenues forming the approaches to temples. The common idea of a Greek Sphinx, on the other hand, is that of a winged body of a lion, the breast and upper part being the figure of a woman. Greek Sphinxes, moreover, are not always represented in lying attitude, but appear in different positions, as it might suit the fancy of the sculptor or poet. Thus they appear with the face of a maiden, the breast, feet and claws of a lion, the tail of a serpent, and the wings of a bird.'[307]

---

[300] Bauer (2007) 110-12.
[301] Although it might be possible that the first Sphinx depicted Queen Hetepheres II, who reigned during the 4th dynasty (2723-2563 B.C.).
[302] Whence the name of the Boeotian mountain, Phikion oros. (Hes. Scut. Herc. 33). Lycophron calls her a Phician monster, mouthing darkly her perplexed words (Lycophron, Alexandra1465, transl. Mair).
[303] Hesiod, Theogony 327.
[304] Apollodorus, Library 3.5, 3.8. Cf. Scholiast on Euripides' Phoenician Women 46.
[305] Scholiast on Euripides, Ion c.
[306] Pausanias claims that the Sphinx was the daughter of Laius (Description of Greece, 9.26.2).
[307] William Smith, A New Classical Dictionary of Greek and Roman Biography, Mythology and Geography, Harper Brothers, New York 1884, p. 831.

Most people would easily associate her with the famous tragic hero Oedipus, whose story became a trademark of world literature by the 5th c. B.C. tragedian Sophocles.[308] After an oracle foretold to Laius, king of ancient Thebes, that his child would cause the death of his father and would marry his mother, Laius sent a servant to kill the child in the woods of mount Cithairon. The servant felt pity for the infant and instead of killing it, hung it from the feet to a tree (according to a different tradition) thus earning him the name Oedipus, which means *swollen feet*. The boy was found by a shepherd and taken to the kingdom of Corinth, where king Polybus and his queen Merope were childless. They brought the baby up as if their own. One day, as is common in these stories, Oedipus found out that he was adopted. Determined to find out his real ancestry he went off to the oracle of Delphi. There he received an oracle saying that if he went back home, he would kill his father and marry his mother.

Despite the fact that in Sophocles' play Oedipus takes so much pride in his superior intellect, he does not think clearly. Because, after this oracle and having found out that Polybus and Merope are not his real parents, he decides to go away from Corinth, fearing that the oracle was about them. As he was leaving the oracle, he came across a rushing chariot with an old man coming the other way on a narrow path. The old man asked him to get out of the path but Oedipus refused. The old man raised his whip to strike him and angered by this gesture Oedipus killed him. The old man was Laius. Oedipus then came to Thebes, to learn that the king had been killed by strangers and the city was plagued by a monster that killed those who attempted to enter Thebes, unless they could answer a riddle.[309] She had sat on the top of a citadel on mount Phicion, outside Thebes, and challenged all passers-by to solve a riddle, otherwise she did not allow them to enter the city.

The famous riddle of the Sphinx was taught to her by the Muses.[310] Others thought that Laius himself had taught her the riddle from the oracles that his father Cadmus had received at Delphi.[311] The answer to the riddle would earn the winner the hand of the recently widowed queen and the throne of Thebes, as proclaimed by the brother of queen Jocasta, Creon, who assumed the role of temporary ruler of Thebes. No one, however, could answer

---

[308] A lost play by Aeschylus was also named Sphinx. It was a satyr play, part of Aeschylus' version of the Oedipus trilogy and it described the encounter of Oedipus with the Sphinx.
[309] Pausanias describes the throne of the temple of Zeus at Olympia and he mentions that 'on each of the two front feet are set Theban children ravished by Sphinxes'. Pausanias, Description of Greece 5.11.2.
[310] Apollodorus, Library 3.5, 3.8.
[311] Pausanias, Description of Greece 9.26.

What is that which has one voice and yet becomes four-footed and two-footed and three-footed?[312]

The famous and simple answer is of course *Man*. Struggling on all fours as a toddler, walking straight on two legs at his prime and three-footed with the aid of a walking stick at old age, Man becomes the triumphant answer and the center of a universe of knowledge and superior intellect.[313] At least this is what Oedipus thought, taking pride in his intelligence that won him a kingdom, a wife and four children by her.

> *I faced the abominable witch though her jaws dripped blood and the ground beneath was white with scattered bones. As she sat on her lofty crag with outstretched wings, waiting to pounce on her prey and lashing her tail like a lion, savage in her wrath, I asked her riddle. A terrible sound rang from above and she snapped her jaws, tearing at the rocks, impatient to claw out my living heart, then spoke her cryptic words and she the baited trap. But the grim riddle of the monstrous bird I solved.*[314]

But Oedipus does not see the truth that is obvious to the blind seer Teiresias, who in vain tries to warn him. When the inevitable truth shone, Oedipus blinded himself as he could no longer look at the sun and the faces of his children who were also his brothers. His mother/wife hung herself and he drove himself into voluntary exile. His two sons, Eteocles and Polynices, who were to rule after him, died from each other's hands simultaneously, fighting for the throne. Whereas his daughter Antigone, was starved to death while imprisoned in the living-tomb of a cave, punished for the attempted burial of her brother who was condemned to stay unburied, because he had betrayed his country. Oedipus did everything wrong: he interpreted the oracle of Delphi incorrectly; he killed an old man without being punished for it, and his hubris was that he thought too much of his own intelligence. For the Greeks, he is a tragic figure, but he was justly destroyed, for the delicate cosmic balance which he upset with his hubristic behavior was restored.

The Sphinx was destroyed long before Oedipus, as soon as he had answered the riddle. She hurled herself down from the citadel where she had been sitting and killed herself.[315] The question, though, is *why was she there initially*? One version has Hera being angry with the Thebans, because they had tolerated a terrible crime: when Laius was young, he was sent to nearby Pisa, where he was offered hospitality

---

[312] Apollodorus, Library 3.5.7.
[313] The riddle is preserved also in Diodorus, Library 4.64.4.
[314] Seneca, Oedipus 91-102 (transl. March).
[315] Hyginus, Fabulae 67.

at the local palace. But, violating every notion of hospitality, he raped and carried off the young prince Chrysippus. Shamed by this, Chrysippus committed suicide. The stain, *miasma*, of this crime caused Hera to send the Sphinx, who came flying from the most distant parts of Ethiopia.[316]

Pausanias tried to rationalize the myth by presenting the Sphinx as a raider who came to the land with pirates, and was destroyed by king Oedipus, or as a daughter of king Laius:

> *Farther on [beyond Thebes, Boiotia] we come to the mountain from which they say the Sphinx, chanting a riddle, sallied to bring death upon those she caught. Others say that roving with a force of ships on a piratical expedition she put in at Anthedon, seized the mountain I mentioned, and used it for plundering raids until Oidipous overwhelmed her by the superior numbers of the army he had with him on his arrival from Korinthos. There is another version of the story which makes her the natural daughter of Laius, who, because he was fond of her, told her the oracle delivered to Kadmos from Delphoi. Now Laius had sons by concubines, and the oracle delivered from Delphoi applied only to Epikaste and her sons. So when any of her brothers came in order to claim the throne from the Sphinx, she resorted to trickery in dealing with them, saying that if they were sons of Laius they should know the oracle that came to Kadmos. When they could not answer she would punish them with death, on the ground that they had no valid claim to the kingdom or to relationship. But Oidipous came because it appears he had been told the oracle in a dream.*[317]

---

[316] Apollodorus, Library and Scholiast on Euripides' Phoenician Women 1760.
[317] Pausanias, Description of Greece 9.26 (transl. Jones).

Chapter 4
Monstrous Animals

The world of the Greeks was surrounded by animals, wild and domesticated. There were animals that helped people with daily tasks, such as plowing or carrying carts, as well as, animals that were used for food or for sacrifices, even pests that destroyed crops or even killed people. Sometimes, myths tell stories about such animals that transcend the ordinary and become potentially or sometimes actually dangerous to people. There are strange kinds of ordinary species, like the Phoenix – a bird with powers that transgress the characteristics of any known kind of fowl – and ordinary animals with exceptional characteristics, such as the wild boar that Hercules had to overcome at mount Erymanthus, in order to complete one of his labors. Monstrosity may be manifested in the world of the usual as well as of the unusual. Monstrous animals are not necessarily frightening or hideous. One does not necessarily detest the sight of a winged horse, like Pegasus; the beautiful horse is a monster, nevertheless, and its parentage strengthens this point.[318]

Cerberus (Κέρβερος)

A kingdom as terrifying as the kingdom of Hades ought to have a fierce guardian. Cerberus was the perfect guardian-dog. He was fathered by the monstrous Typhon and Echidna[319] – and this made him the sibling of many other famous creatures, such as the Hydra of Lerna, the Chimaera and Orthus. He became very popular in art, especially vase paintings of the archaic and classical period; especially popular was the part of the story which has Hercules bringing the dog back to Mycenae and the coward king Euyrustheus jumps terrified into a big jar half-buried in the ground. Hercules would have never accomplished this task, without divine help, especially Athena's. In book 8 of the *Iliad*, Athena complains about Zeus, who does not allow Hector to be killed, and she reminds us of the precious help she offered to Zeus' favorite son, Hercules, during his labors commanded by his cousin, Eurystheus:

---

[318] According to tradition, Medusa was impregnated by Poseidon, and when Perseus decapitated Medusa, Pegasus and Chrysaor (father of the monstrous Geryon) sprang out of here body. Hesiod believes that Pegasus' name (pege= spring) is inspired by the place of its birth, which is associated with the springs of the Ocean (Hesiod, Theogony 281-286; Apollodorus II, 3, 4).

[319] Hesiod, Theogony 310; Quintus Smyrnaeus 6.260; Hyginus, Fabulae, 30. Bacchhylides (frag. 5) and Ovid (Metamorphoses 7.412) name only Echidna.

*...nor remembers all those many times I rescued his own son,
Herakles, when the tasks of Eurystheus were too much for his strength.
And time and time again he would cry out aloud to the heavens,
and Zeus would send me down in speed from the sky to help him.
If in the wiliness of my heart I had had thoughts like his,
When Herakles was sent down to Hades of the Gates, to hale back
from the kingdom of the Dark the hound of the grisly death god,
never would he have got clear of the steep-dripping Stygian water.*[320]

The appearance of the dog is not consistent in literary and archaeological sources. A beautiful Caeretan black-figure hydria dated from the 6th c. B.C. now kept in the Louvre, Paris, depicts Hercules presenting Cerberus to Eurystheus, who is already hiding in a *pithos*, a big storage jar, half-buried in the ground. Cerberus is drawn with three heads, and snakes are growing from the heads of the dog and its front paws. Homer does not describe it in detail;[321] in both the *Iliad* and the *Odyssey* the monster is referred to only as the dog of Hades and it is not even mentioned by name. Hesiod's *Theogony* is the oldest surviving extant literary source that names him Cerberus. In this version, he is described as a dog with fifty heads: 'and then again she bore a second, a monster not to be overcome and that may not be described, Cerberus who eats raw flesh, the brazen-voiced hound of Hades, fifty-headed, relentless and strong.'[322] The number of the heads tends to shrink in later literary tradition. When it comes to art, Cerberus is often depicted with just one or two heads, but most writers attribute three terrible heads to it.[323] The unnatural form is enhanced by the addition of a serpent-tail and a mane of snakes with venomous heads.[324] Eyes sparkling with flashes complete the terrifying portrait.[325]

---

[320] Homer, Iliad 8. 362-369 (transl. Lattimore).
[321] 'But Homer, who was the first to call the creature brought by Herakles the Hound of Hades, did not give it a name or describe it as of manifold form, as he did the Khimaira (Chimera). Late poets gave it the name Kerberos, and though in other respects they made him resemble a dog, they say that he had three heads. Homer, however, does not imply that he was a dog, the friend of man, any more than if he called a real serpent the Hound of Hades'. Pausanias, Description of Greece, 3.25.5-7 (transl. Jones).
[322] Hesiod, Theogony 309-11 (transl. Evelyn-White).
[323] Perhaps the snakes that grew from the head and paws of the dog in early art confused later writers, who described the dog as fifty-headed (Hesiod, Theogony 311).
[324] Apollodorus, 2. 5.12; Euripides, Hercules 24, 611; Virgil, Aeneid 7.417; Ovid, Metamorphoses 4.449).
[325] Euphorion, Fragments III, no 121.

Hercules, Cerberus and Eurystheus. c. 525 B.C., Museum of Louvre. By Eagle Painter (User:Bibi Saint-Pol, Own work, 1 June 2007) [Public domain], via Wikimedia Commons

The job of this monster was to guard the entrance to the underworld, which the Greeks placed at the south of the Peloponnese, at cape Taenarum.[326] According to Hesiod, not only does he prevent people escaping from the underworld, but he eats them up, if they try to flee back to life:' A fearful hound guards the house in

---

[326] The actual entrance to the underworld is problematic even by mythological standards. After Hercules left the realm of Hades he passed from the Acherousia lake, through which the river Acheron flowed (Thucydides 1. 46; Strabo, 7. 324). This lake is in Thesprotia. Acheron is one of the five rivers that flow in the underworld. Their names are: Styx (the river of hate), Acheron (river of sorrow), Cocytus (river of lamentation), Lethe (river of forgetfulness) and Pyriphlegethon (river of fire). See, Homer, Iliad 4,10ff, Odyssey 10.513; Sappho, fragment 95; Aeschylus, Agamemnon 1156ff, Alcestis, 439ff; Plato, Phaedo 112e (who mentions Ocean, as the outer river); Apollonius Rhodius, Argonautica, 1, 642, 2.726; Pausanias, Description of Greece 10.28.1ff; Virgil, Aeneid, 6.323ff; Propertius, Elegies 4.7; Seneca, Hercules Furens, 709ff, 726ff, Oedipus 575ff, Phaedra 93ff; Apuleius, The Golden Ass 6.18ff; Nonnus, Dionysiaca 17.300ff; Suidas, s.v. Akherousia, Akheron.

front, pitiless, and he has a cruel trick. To those who go in, he fawns with his tail and both his ears; prevents them from going out back again, but keeps watch and devours whomever he catches going out of the gates of strong Hades and awful Persephone'.[327]

This was the monster that Hercules was ordered, by his cousin Eurystheus, to bring back from the kingdom of the dead.[328] For Apollodorus, bravery was not an issue here, since it was taken for granted, but there were other problems to be solved. Entering the realm of the dead meant that Hercules had to prepare himself first, by partaking at the Eleusinian mysteries and being initiated. The problem was that only Athenians could be initiated there, and thus it was suggested that he was adopted by an Athenian named Pylius.[329] 'But not being able to see the mysteries because he had not been cleansed of the slaughter of the centaurs, he was cleansed by Eumolpus and then initiated'.[330]

Once the complex problem of nationality and admittance to religious cults was solved, Hercules found the entrance of the underworld at cape Taenarum in Laconia, in the south of the Peloponnese.[331] By the 5th c. B.C. it was clear – and perhaps, potentially funny – that Hercules was successful in bringing the dog above

---

[327] Hesiod, Theogony 769-74.

[328] The sequence of Heracles' labors varies considerably in antiquity. Cf. Graves (2002) vol. 2, 472-3. Nevertheless, the descent of Hercules to the underworld is always the last of these labors and it probably stands for the emergence of the hero from death and his way to the ultimate apotheosis, his deification.

[329] Apollodorus, Library 2.5. As to the initiation of Herakles at Eleusis, compare Diod. 4.25.1; Tzetzes, Chiliades ii.394. According to Diodorus, the rites were performed on this occasion by Musaeus, son of Orpheus. Elsewhere (Tzetzes, Chiliades iv.14.3) the same writer says that Demeter instituted the lesser Eleusinian mysteries in honour of Herakles for the purpose of purifying him after his slaughter of the centaurs. The statement that Pylius acted as adoptive father to Herakles at his initiation is repeated by Plutarch, Theseus. 33, who mentions that before Castor and Pollux were initiated at Athens they were in like manner adopted by Aphidnus. Herodotus (8.65) says that any Greek who pleased might be initiated at Eleusis. The initiation of Herakles is represented in ancient reliefs (note from Perseus.tufts.edu).

[330] Apollodorus, Library 2.5. Cf. Diodorus, Library 4.25.1, who names Musaios, the son of Orpheus, as the priest who was in charge of the initiatory rituals at the time.

[331] According to another account, Herakles descended, not at Taenarum but at the Acherusian Chersonese, near Heraclea Pontica on the Black Sea. The marks of the descent were there pointed out to a great depth (Pausanias, Description of Greece, 3.25. 5-7); also, Xenophon, Anabasis 6.2.2. Cf. Strabo, Geography 8. 5. 1: 'A headland that projects into the sea, Tainaron, with its temple of Poseidon situated in a grove; and secondly, nearby, to the cavern through which, according to the myth writers, Kerberos (Cerberus) was brought up from Haides by Herakles' (transl. Jones).

the surface.³³² From the 5th c. B.C. poet Bacchylides, we learn that Hercules was encountered by the souls of the dead, dueling near the river Cocytus.³³³ The souls fled away in fear, when they saw the fierce hero. According to Apollodorus, only two souls did not cower away from him, the soul of the hero Meleager and the soul of the Gorgon Medusa. Hercules drew his sword against the Gorgon, as if she were alive. There he met with Hermes, the messenger of the gods who has the ability to cross boundaries, especially the boundaries between the world of the living and of the immortals. As a matter of fact, Hermes was authorized to be there, since he was also the famous Soul-Bearer, the *psychopompos*, who leads the souls of the dead to the afterlife.³³⁴ Hermes saw Hercules trying in vain to hit the ghost of Medusa and advised him to stop, since it was only 'an empty phantom'.³³⁵ After this encounter, Hercules came across Meleager. The latter was so impressed when he saw Hercules alive in the underworld, that he offered to him his sister as his wife. The girl's name was Deianeira, 'upon whose neck was still the green of youth, nor did she know yet of the ways of Aphrodite, charmer of men'.³³⁶ Hercules will emerge from the world of the dead with yet another trophy, a wife, although unknowingly he secures himself a ticket to return to death: Deianeira will be literally the death of him, since she will poison him, albeit unintentionally, with the blood of the centaur Nessus.³³⁷

More interesting encounters await Hercules on his way to Cerberus. Once deep in the underworld, he came across Theseus and Peirithous who were on two thrones permanently fixed in the sitting position. Theseus, the future king of Athens and his best friend had made a pact: they would help each other kidnap the woman they wanted to marry, and both of them wanted to marry daughters of Zeus.³³⁸ Theseus chose first, and he chose Helen – later known as the *Helen of Troy*. She was kidnapped and kept until she would become of the right age to marry, although she was returned to her family by the Dioscouri, before this marriage took place.³³⁹ Then it was Peirithous' turn. He chose Persephone. The two friends managed to

---

³³² Aristophanes, Peace 315ff and especially Frogs 468ff, not only mention Cerberus, but present him like a pet being stolen from its master.
³³³ Baccylides, Fragment 5.
³³⁴ Apollodorus, Library, 2.5.
³³⁵ Apollodorus, Library, 2.5. Apollodorus is right, of course, in naming only one ghost of the three Gorgons, since Medusa was the only mortal one. Cf. Apollodorus. 2.4.2. Compare Homer, Odyssey 11.634ff.
³³⁶ Bacchylides, Epinician Ode 5. 172-5 (transl. Morford & Lenardon).
³³⁷ Cf. the version recorded in Euripides' 5th c. B.C. play Hercules.
³³⁸ Scholia on Iliad 3.144 and a fragment (#227) of Pindar, according to Kerenyi 1951:237, note 588.
³³⁹ Athenaeus, Deipnosophistai 13.4 (557a).

go down to the underworld but they were caught by Hades, who made them sit on seats from which they could never rise. Hercules managed to rescue Theseus, yet every time he tried to raise Peirithous from his seat, a great earthquake shook the cave.[340] They had to abandon him and he must be still there, causing earthquakes with every effort to escape.

Hercules went deeper into the cave of Hades and he saw the animal:

> And the snakes under his shaggy belly,
> the snakes of his belly licked their tongues on his ribs
> and in his eyes a dark flash was shining.
> Indeed, in the Forges or somewhere at Meligouni,[341] such
> sparks were emitted when iron was worked with hammers
> and the well-beaten anvil roared,
> or inside smoky Aetna, lair of Asteropos.
> And he came to Tiryns to the evil Eurystheus
> Alive, returning from Hades, the last of his twelve labors;
> and at the triple crossroads of Mideia
> trembling in fear, women with their children looked upon him.[342]

The animal is extraordinary, but so is Hercules. Not only for his unprecedented strength and his labors, but mainly because of his evolution, as it is implied by his labors. Despite the often inconsistent order of their accomplishment,[343] it is commonly accepted that the first six of his labors take place in the Peloponnese (namely, the killing of the Nemean Lion, the extermination of the Hydra of Lerna, the capture of Artemis' deer, the cleansing of Augeas' stables and the killing of the Stymphalian birds) and establish Hercules as a local hero. After these, Hercules travels from the most southern part of Greece, Crete, in order to bring back the bull of Minos (the father of the Minotaur), to the most northern part of Greece, Thrace, in order to bring back the man-eating mares of king Diomedes; thus Hercules becomes a Pan-Hellenic hero. For his eighth mission, he travels to the Black Sea, to the land of the Amazons, to steal the belt of queen Hippolyta. Then he goes to the Ocean, to steal the cattle of Geryon and then, searching for someone to guide him

---

[340] Diodorus (Library 4.25.1) writes that Hercules rescued both of them.
[341] A place mentioned by Callimachus in his Hymns, and by Lycophron in his Alexandra.
[342] Euphorion, Fragments III, no 121 (transl. Syropoulos). The ancient Greek text is from TLG 2002 A.
[343] For example, Diodorus places the descent to the underworld and the kidnapping of Cerberus, before the quest for the apples of the Hesperides, which according to him, is the last of his labors.

to the land of the Hesperides, he travels from Asia to Africa and then somewhere out of the Mediterranean; thus he becomes an international hero. Hercules travels everywhere, and he always returns with a trophy – perhaps something to symbolize the unending passion of the Greeks for travelling abroad, expanding their land, their economy and their culture. Hercules' ultimate descent is down to Hades. He emerges with the ultimate trophy, proof that he went there and back: Cerberus. Man triumphs over death. He becomes a cosmic hero; and one might think that this is the height of evolution: from local, to national, to international, to cosmic hero! But there is more. At the end of his life, Hercules, losing his life because of his wife Deianeira, will be put on a pyre and rescued by Athena in the nick of time, only to be brought to Olympus and become immortal.[344] Hercules' deification, his *apotheosis*, is the peak of evolution: from mortal to immortal; from man to beyond humanity. No other hero has accomplished anything like this.[345] He transgressed every known and unchartered boundary, geographical or mythical, and became a god. Even Achilles, who seems to enjoy privileges of a leading officer amongst the souls in the underworld and impresses Odysseus who also descended in the kingdom of Hades in the *Odyssey*, is not immortal.[346] He is dead. It is a far different status, compared to what Hercules gets at the end of his life.

The details about Hercules' struggle with Cerberus have been recorded by many different writers. As with other occasions, when Hercules had to overcome an animal that belonged to a god (i.e. the deer of Artemis), he had to get the permission of the owner before subduing it. In the 1st c. B.C. Diodorus wrote that Hercules was 'welcomed like a brother' by Persephone, who allowed him to get the dog, if he could catch him without hurting him. So, 'by the favor of Persephone' he accomplished the task and carried Cerberus up to the light in chains, to the amazement of all 'and exhibited him to men'.[347] . Plutarch, *Life of Nisias* 1.3, also confirms that it was Persephone who helped him by delivering Cerberus into his hands, while Hyginus claims that it was the Fates, who allowed him to mess with the balance between life and death and take to the light the symbol of the

---

[344] Cf. Euripides, Hercules and Ovid, Isthmian 4.61-7.
[345] One might take this further and consider Hercules himself as a monster: his excessive strength and his accomplishments certainly transgress human limits and limitations and any sense of what is ordinary.
[346] In Odyssey 11. 485-490, Odysseus uses the verb κρατέειν (to rule), to describe Achilles' status among the dead, and Achilles responds by using the verb ἀνάσσειν (to reign): 485 Ἀργεῖοι, νῦν αὖτε μέγα κρατέεις νεκύεσσιν/ ἐνθάδ' ἐών· τῷ μή τι θανὼν ἀκαχίζευ, Ἀχιλλεῦ.'/ 'ὣς ἐφάμην, ὁ δέ μ' αὐτίκ' ἀμειβόμενος προσέειπε· /'μὴ δή μοι θάνατόν γε παραύδα, φαίδιμ' Ὀδυσσεῦ./ βουλοίμην κ' ἐπάρουρος ἐὼν θητευέμεν ἄλλῳ, /490 ἀνδρὶ παρ' ἀκλήρῳ, ᾧ μὴ βίοτος πολὺς εἴη,/ἢ πᾶσιν νεκύεσσι καταφθιμένοισιν ἀνάσσειν.
[347] Diodorus, Library 4.25.1

inescapability from death.[348] The ascent of the dog to the light is eloquently described by the Latin poet Ovid, who pictured him 'dragged struggling, blinking, screwing up his eyes against the sunlight and the blinding day, the hell-hound Cerberus, fast on a chain of adamant. His three throats filled the air with triple barking, barks of frenzied rage, and spattered the green meadows with white spume'.[349] The same picture of Cerberus who is at first tamed by Hercules, but then startled by the light of day, to which he is not accustomed, is found also in the Latin tragedy *Hercules Furens*, by Seneca.[350]

The Romans could not but be mesmerized by a wonderful myth like this. In his *Metamorphoses* Ovid describes how the foam from the mouth of Cerberus became a powerful poison, equal to the venom of Echidna, used by the Fury (Erinys) Tisiphone to invoke madness.[351] According to him, when Cerberus' spittle was shed on to the ground, aconite flourished -- a poisonous plant of the buttercup family, which bears hooded pink or purple flowers. This Medea used as poison, convincing Aegeus to offer it to his son, Theseus.[352]

Hercules was not the only hero associated with the taming of Cerberus. Orpheus and Aeneas had to confront it, too. Orpheus, one of the four mortals who went alive to the underworld and came out of it again,[353] had to subdue Cerberus when he went to the kingdom of Hades to get his wife, Eurydice back. Unlike Hercules, Orpheus did not possess any special lion-hide, to protect him from the bites of Cerberus' snakes, or supernatural strength to wrestle it. However, Cerberus could not resist the compelling power of music of Orpheus' lyre.[354] As for Aeneas, Virgil describes how the Sibyl of the temple of Apollo at Cumae advised him how to go

---

[348] Hyginus, Fabulae 251.
[349] Ovid, Metamorphoses 7.142.
[350] Seneca, Hercules Furens 598, 782 ff.
[351] Ovid, Metamorphoses 4.500 ff.
[352] Ovid, Metamorphoses 7.142.
[353] They are Odysseus, Hercules, Orpheus and Aeneas. One might add Sisyphus, the king of Ephyra. He advised his wife Merope to bury him without the appropriate rites, perhaps without the coin to pay the ferryman of the dead. Hades let him go back to reproach his wife and he simply never returned. When he died for a second time, in old age, he was punished for all eternity, condemned to roll a great boulder on a hill, only to see it roll down the slope before he reached the top. See, Homer, Iliad 6.152-5; Pindar, Olympian 13.52; Apollodorus, Argonautica 1.7.3, 1.9.3, 3.4.3, 3.10.1, 3.12.6; Pausanias, Description of Greece 2.1.3, 2.2.2., 2.3.11, 2.4.3, 2.5.1, 10.31.10.
[354] Pindar, Pythian 4.176-7; Aeschylus, Agamemnon 1629-30; Euripides, Bacchae 560-4, Iphigeneia at Aulis 1211-14; Plato, Symposium 179 b-d; Apollonius, Argonautica; Apollodorus 1.3.2, 1.9.16, 1.9.25, 2.4.9; Diodorus, Library 1.23, 1.96, 3.65, 4.25; Virgil, Georgics 4.453-503; Ovid, Metamorphoses 10.1-85, 11.1-84.

past Cerberus, in order to find the spirit of his father Anchises and consult him about the settlement of the Trojans in Latium. This time a honey-cake dipped in pacifying drugs is used to put Cerberus off-guard for a while.[355]

Orthus (Ὄρθος)

Orthus (sometimes found as Orthrus)[356] is a brother to Cerberus[357] and the Chimaera, fathered by Typhon and Echidna[358] and as such he also possesses unnatural characteristics. As with Cerberus, there is no consistency in depictions of him in art, so we usually come across him presented with two heads, but often with three or only one. He was the father of other monsters, such as the Sphinx and the Lion of Nemea.[359] Although it is not very clear in the text of the *Theogony*, it seems that the mother of these two monsters was Orthus' own mother, Echidna.

Hercules faced this monstrous dog while trying to steal the cattle of Geryon. Geryon was a monster himself being the son of the giant Chrysaor and the sea-nymph Callirhoe. He was the strongest of all men,[360] and he had three torsos, three heads and three pairs of hands on two stout feet. He lived on the island of Erytheia, meaning *red land*, somewhere in the west, beyond the river Ocean (sometimes the location is identified with Sicily). His cattle were famous for their beautiful reddish hide and king Eurystheus of Mycenae commanded Hercules to bring the valuable animals to him.[361]

---

[355] Virgil, Aeneid 6.417-25. The cake is offered simply as a distraction in the version of Apuleius' The Golden Ass 6.19ff: you must disarm him by offering him a cake as his spoils. Then you can easily pass him, and gain immediate access to Proserpina herself... When you have obtained what she gives you, you must make your way back, using the remaining cake to neutralize the dog's savagery.

[356] Quintus Smyrnaeus, Posthomerica vi.253 (Orthros); Scholiast on Pind. I. 1.13(15) (Orthos); Scholiast on Plat. Tim. 24e (Orthros, so Stallbaum); Tzetzes, Chiliades ii.333 (Orthros); Pediasmus, De Herculis laboribus 10 (Orthos); Serv. Verg. A. 8.300 (Orthrus).

[357] As stressed by Quintus Smyrnaeus, Fall of Troy 6. 249 ff: Before him slain lay that most murderous hound Orthros, in furious might like Cerberus, his brother-hound.

[358] Hesiod, Theogony 309; Apollodorus 2.106; Quintus Smyrnaeus 6.249, 260.

[359] Hesiod, Theogony 326-32.

[360] Hesiod, Theogony 981.

[361] Hesiod, Theogony 287-94, 979-83; Pindar, fr. 169a; Aeschylus, Agamemnon 870-3; Herodotus 4.8l Apollodorus 2.5.10; Pausanias, 1.35.7-8, 3.18.13; Virgil, Aeneid 6.289 (Frazer's notes)

MONSTROUS ANIMALS   93

A two-headed Orthrus, with snake tail, lying wounded at the feet of Heracles (left) and the three-bodied Geryon (right). Detail from a red-figure kylix by Euphronios, 550–500 BC, Staatliche Antikensammlungen (Munich 2620).

As a tenth labour he was ordered to fetch the cattle of Geryon from Erythia. Now Erythia was an island near the ocean; it is now called Gadira.[362] *This island was inhabited by Geryon, son of Chrysaor by Callirrhoe, daughter of Ocean. He had the body of three men grown together and joined in one at the waist, but parted in three from the flanks and thighs. He owned red kine, of which Eurytion was the herdsman and Orthus, the two-headed hound, begotten by Typhon on Echidna, was the watchdog. So journeying through Europe to fetch the kine of Geryon he destroyed many wild beasts and set foot in Libya, and proceeding to Tartessus he erected as tokens of his journey two pillars over against each other at the boundaries of Europe and Libya.*[363] *But being heated by the Sun on his journey, he*

---

[362] Compare Hdt. 4.8; Strab. 3.2.11, Strab. 3.5 4; Pliny, Nat. Hist. iv.120; Solinus xxiii.12. Gadira is Cadiz. According to Pliny, Nat. Hist. iv.120, the name is derived from a Punic word gadir, meaning 'hedge.' Compare Dionysius, Perieg. 453ff. The same word agadir is still used in the south of Morocco in the sense of 'fortified house,' and many places in that country bear the name. Amongst them the port of Agadir is the best known. See E. Doutté, En tribu (Paris, 1914), pp. 50ff. The other name of the island is given by Solinus xxiii.12 in the form Erythrea, and by Mela iii.47 in the form Eythria (Frazer's notes)

[363] The opinions of the ancients were much divided on the subject of the Pillars of

> bent his bow at the god, who in admiration of his hardihood, gave him a golden goblet in which he crossed the ocean. And having reached Erythia he lodged on Mount Abas. However the dog, perceiving him, rushed at him; but he smote it with his club, and when the herdsman Eurytion came to the help of the dog, Hercules killed him too. But Menoetes, who was there pasturing the kine of Hades, reported to Geryon what had occurred, and he, coming up with Hercules beside the river Anthemus,[364] as he was driving away the kine, joined battle with him and was shot dead. And Hercules, embarking the kine in the goblet and sailing across to Tartessus, gave back the goblet to the Sun.[365]

So, according to Apollodorus, Hercules killed the two herdsmen, Eurytion and Menoetes, the dog Orthus and Geryon himself. The cattle were brought to Mycenae where Eurystheus sacrificed them to Hera.

Herakles. See Strab. 3.5.5. The usual opinion apparently identified them with the rock of Calpe (Gibraltar) and the rock of Abyla, Abila, or Abylica (Ceuta) on the northern and southern sides of the straits. See Strab. 3.5.5; Tzetzes, Scholiast on Lycophron 649; Pliny, Nat. Hist. iii.4; Mela i.27, ii.95; Martianus Capella vi.624. Further, it seems to have been commonly supposed that before the time of Herakles the two continents were here joined by an isthmus, and that the hero cut through the isthmus and so created the straits. See Diod. 4.18.5; Seneca, Herakles Furens 235ff.; Seneca, Herakles Oetaeus 1240; Pliny, Nat. Hist. iii.4; Pliny, Nat. Hist. iii.4; Mela i.27; Martianus Capella vi.625. Some people, however, on the contrary, thought that the straits were formerly wider, and that Herakles narrowed them to prevent the monsters of the Atlantic ocean from bursting into the Mediterranean (Diod. 4.18.5). An entirely different opinion identified the Pillars of Herakles with two brazen pillars in the sanctuary of Herakles at Gadira (Cadiz), on which an inscription was engraved recording the cost of building the temple. See Strab. 3.5.5; compare Pliny, Nat. Hist. ii.242, who speaks of 'the columns of Herakles consecrated at Gadira.' For other references to the Pillars of Herakles, see Pind. O. 3.43ff., Pind. N. 3.21, Pind. I. 4.11ff..; Athenaeus vii.98, p. 315 CD; Tzetzes, Chiliades ii.339 (who here calls the pillars Alybe and Abinna); Scholiast on Plat. Tim. 24e; Dionysius of Halicarnassus, Orbis Descriptio 64-68, with the commentary of Eustathius (Geographi Graeci Minores, ed. C. Müller, ii. pp. 107, 228). According to Eustathius, Calpe was the name given to the rock of Gibraltar by the barbarians, but its Greek name was Alybe; and the rock of Ceuta was called Abenna by the barbarians but by the Greeks Cynegetica, that is, the Hunter's Rock. He tells us further that the pillars were formerly named the Pillars of Cronus, and afterwards the Pillars of Briareus.
[364] Compare Tzetzes, Scholiast on Lycophron 652, who probably follows Apollodorus (Frazer's notes).
[365] Apollodorus, Library 2.5.10 (transl. Frazer).

Many vase-paintings from around 510-500 B.C. (like a beautiful attic red-figure cylix, signed by the painter Euphronius, now kept at Munich) depict Orthus dead at the feet of Hercules, pierced by arrows; his twin heads and his serpent tail are obvious. Apollodorus, however, reports that the dog was not shot with arrows but clubbed to death by Hercules.[366]

Mares of Diomedes (Διομήδου Ἵπποι)

The eighth labor of Hercules brought him to Thrace in northern Greece. Eurystheus commanded Hercules to bring the famous horses of Diomedes, the king of the local Bistones, back to Myceneae. Diomedes was the son of the god of war, Ares and the nymph Cyrene.[367] Hyginus attributed his parentage to the Titan Atlas and his own daughter, Asteria.[368]

Owing, perhaps, to the warlike nature of his father, Diomedes was a savage king. He decorated the wall of his palace with the skulls of his victims,[369] whose flesh he fed to his horses.[370] According to Hyginus, the horses' names were Podagrus (Wild Feet), Lampon (The Bright One), Xanthus (the Fair/Blonde) and Deinus (The Terrible).[371] They were kept chained with iron bonds to the stables, and their bronze mangers were always stained with the blood of the kings' enemies.[372]

In Euripides' *Hercules* it is stated that Hercules did not go to Thrace to merely steal the horses, but the whole of the four-horse chariot of Diomedes:

> *Heracles*
> *Strangers, citizens of this land of Pherae, do I find Admetus at home?*
>
> *Chorus-Leader*
> *Yes, Pheres' son is at home, Heracles. But tell us what need brings you to* <u>Thessaly</u> *[480] and to this city of Pherae.*
>
> *Heracles*
> *I am performing a certain labor for Eurystheus, king of* <u>Tiryns</u>.

---

[366] Apollodorus 2.5.10.
[367] Apollodorus, Library 2.5, 2.8.; Pausanias, Description of Greece 3.18.12; Diodorus, Library 4.15.3-4; Quintus Smyrnaeus, Fall of Troy 6.270ff, et.al.
[368] Huginus, Fabulae 250.
[369] Ovid, Heroides 9.87ff.
[370] Apollodrus, Library 2.5.8; Diodorus, Library 4.15.3-4; Ovid, Heroides 9.69ff, 9.87ff; Seneca, Hercules Oetaeus 18ff; Quintus Smyrnaeus, Fall of Troy 6.270ff. Seneca, in his Troades 1106ff implies that even babies were fed to the mares.
[371] Hyginus, Fabulae 30.
[372] Diodorus, Library 4.15-3-4.

Chorus-Leader
Where are you bound? What is the wandering you are constrained to make?

Heracles
I go in quest of the four-horse chariot of Thracian Diomedes.

Chorus-Leader
How can you do that? Do you not know what kind of host he is?

Heracles
[485] I do not. I have never yet been to Bistonia.

Chorus-Leader
You cannot possess those horses without a fight.

Heracles
But all the same, I cannot decline these labors.

Chorus-Leader
Then you will either kill him and return or end your days there.

Heracles
This is not the first such race I shall have run.

Chorus-Leader
[490] If you defeat their master, what will it profit you?

Heracles
I will bring the horses back to the lord of Tiryns.

Chorus-Leader
You will not find it easy to put a bit in their mouths.

Heracles
Surely so, unless they breathe fire from their nostrils.

Chorus-Leader
No, but they tear men apart with their nimble jaws.

Heracles
[495] This is fodder for mountain beasts, not horses.

Chorus-Leader
You will see their feeding-troughs drenched with blood.

Heracles
Whose son does their master claim to be?

Chorus-Leader
Ares' son, and shield-bearing lord of Thrace, rich in gold.

Heracles
Like the others this labor you name befits my destiny [500] (which is always hard and steep) since I am fated to do battle with all the sons of Ares: first Lycaon, then Cycnus, and now this is the third contest I enter, going off to fight horses and master alike. [505] But no one shall ever see Alcmene's son quake at the hand of an enemy.[373]

In this version of Hercules, the hero arrived at Thrace alone, although later sources describe a proper expedition with an army of volunteers.[374] Apollodorus informs us that Hercules had to overpower an unknown number of grooms who were in charge of the stables. Then Hercules drove the horses to the sea, in order to embark them on ships and carry them back to Mycenae. In this version, the king with an army of Bistones came to the rescue of the horses. While preparing for fight, Hercules entrusted the mares to his minion Abderus, a son of Hermes, who lived at Opus in Locris, Thessaly. Hercules and his men fought hard and Diomedes was killed during the ensuing battle. Unfortunately, during the fight the horses turned against Abderus and killed him. On his return,

Hercules and the Mares of Diomedes. Detail of The Twelve Labours Roman mosaic from Llíria, between 201-250 AD (Valencia, Spain).

---
[373] Euripides, Hercules 479-506 (transl. Kovacs).
[374] Apollodorus, Library 2.5.8.

Hercules found his dismembered body and to honor his friend he founded the city of Abdera there. The horses were brought to Eurystheus, but he let them go free. The animals came to mount Olympus, where they were eaten by wild animals – thus bringing some sense of balance to the distraction they caused all this time.[375]

The nature of the animals was intentionally distorted by their master, who taught them how to eat human flesh. After Hercules had defeated Diomedes, he fed his flesh to the horses that were now tamed and became normal. Hercules, then, led them to Mycenae, where Eurystheus received them and consecrated them to Hera. According to this version by Diodorus, the mares' breed continued down to the reign of Alexander the Great of Macedonia.[376]

In the 3rd c. A.D., Philostratus suggested that the four mares were clubbed to death by Hercules, alongside their – ever more monstrous – master: '...he crushed them with his club – one of them lies on the ground, another is gasping for breath, a third, you will say, is leaping up, another is falling down; their manes are unkempt, they are shaggy down to their hoofs, and in every way they resemble wild beasts; their stalls are tainted with the flesh and bones of the men whom Diomedes used as food for his horses, and the breeder of the mares himself is even more savage of aspect than the mares near whom he has fallen'.[377]

Despite the exciting story, not many vase paintings preserve the memory of this labor of Hercules.

Lion of Nemea (Λέων Νεμέας)

Despite their prominence in ancient Greek art, lions seem to never have roamed ancient Greece. Osteo-archaeology studies the remains of humans and animals of the past. The resilient substance of teeth and claws allows them to survive for thousands of years. Research has revealed the existence of predators such as bears and even wolves in Greece, still to be found in northern Greece, but never lions.[378] Herodotus reports stories of lions to have lived in Greece in historic times,[379] but Herodotus is not the most reliable of sources and he has often been caught exaggerating or distorting information.[380] Recent zoological research

---

[375] Apollodorus, Library 2.5.8; Diodorus, Library 4. 15; Hyginus, Fabulae 30; Euripides, Alcestis 483, 493, Hercules 380; Ptolemy Hephaestion 5.
[376] Diodorus, Library 4.15.3-4.
[377] Philostratus the Elder, Imagines 2.25.
[378] Bears are often found in Greek myths (e.g. the myth of Callisto). Wolves are more rare, but they are also mentioned by writers (e.g. in Theocritus' Idyll 25, Hercules wishes that he will meet the lion of Nemea before the 'cursed breed of wolves').
[379] Sallares (1991) 140.
[380] Amayor O. K., 'Did Herodotus ever go to Egypt?', Journal of the American Research Center

concludes that lions ceased inhabiting Europe since the extinction of the cave lion in prehistoric times.[381] However, from the lions that guard the island of Delos or the entrance to the citadel of Mycenae, to the famous Macedonian lion-sculpture at Chaeronea, to the recently dug tomb at Amphipolis (summer 2014) and the mosaic of Alexander's lion hunt, found at Pella (325-300 B.C.), this animal fascinated Greek imagination. Perhaps they invaded myths after the Greeks had come in contact with the Egyptians and the East, through the stories of travelers and mercenaries who returned home from abroad. As for researchers, such as Aristotle (4th c. B.C., *De Anima*), they would have extensive information brought from Persia, which had links with Africa. The lion is a monster in itself. A huge mane around

Herakles and the Nemean Lion. Attic white-ground black-figured oinochoe, ca. 520-500 BC. From Vulci.

a massive head, overwhelming power and lethal claws ... it would not take much more for this creature to pass into the pantheon of monstrosity. Pretty much like the dragons that guarded the medieval castles of Britain, lions did not have to be real in order to be part of Greek mythology.

---

in Egypt, Vol. 15 (1978) 59-73; Waters, K. H.,. Herodotos the Historian: His Problems, Methods, and Originality. Norman, University of Oklahoma Press, 1985. Introduction. Also, Pipes, David, Herodotus: Father of History, Father of Lies, http://www.loyno.edu/~history/journal/1998-9/Pipes.htm.

[381] Yamaguchi, Nobuyuki; Cooper, Alan; Werdelin, Lars; MacDonald, David W. (2004). 'Evolution of the mane and group-living in the lion (Panthera leo): a review'. Journal of Zoology 263 (4): 329.

One of the most notorious lions in ancient Greek myths is the lion that Hercules had to subdue after Eurystheus commanded him to do so. According to most versions, this was the first of the hero's great adventures, which gave him the symbol that was meant to characterize him for all eternity: the lion-skin.

In Hesiod's *Theogony*, we read that the lion was an offspring of Orthus, the dog fathered by Typhon, and Echidna.[382] Apollodorus makes Typhon the father of the lion.[383] Later writers such as Aelian (2nd c. A.D.) considered Selene, the moon, the mother of this beast. She gave birth to it at the bidding of Hera.[384] Many writers agree that this was Hera's first attempt to dispose of Hercules as an adult, as the lion was especially reared by Hera to destroy him.[385] According to Callimachus (3rd c. B.C.), Hera used the lion both to destroy Argos, despite the fact that Argos was a portion of land allotted to her, and to destroy Hercules.[386] Always communicating her wishes to Eurystheus in an unspecified manner – gods could easily communicate with mortals via dreams, revelations, oracles or direct orders – Hera had her loudspeaker, king of Mycenae, send Hercules to this mission-impossible. It was his first adventure to the land of Peloponnese.[387]

The lion lived on the hills of Nemea and plagued the people who lived around this area, which included Mounts Tretos and Apesas.[388] Its lair was a cave with two entrances[389] near the grove of Nemean Zeus.[390] Nemea was a 'well-watered

---

[382] Hesiod, Theogony 327.
[383] Apollodorus, Library, 2.74.
[384] Aelian, On Animals 12.7. who draws from a tradition recorded by Epimenides. He also records a tradition which claims that the animal fell from the moon. Same in Hyginus, Fabulae 30, who is not clear on whether the Moon (Luna) gave birth to the lion, but it definitely suckled or nourished it. Cf. Bacchylides, fragment 9: The luxuriant ground of Nemeian Zeus, where white-armed Hera nurtured the sheep-killing deep-voiced lion, first of Herakles' glorious contests. Same in Callimachus' fragment 108 (from a Scholiast on Pindar's Nemean Ode 10.1): [The Nemean Lion] to whom [Hera] the wrathful spouse of Zeus gave Argos to keep, albeit it was her own possession, to the end that it might be a stern labour for [Herakles] the bastard offspring of Zeus.
[385] The first attempt was when he was still an infant in his cradle and he killed the two serpents that were sent by Hera to kill him (Theocritus, Idylls 19-25; Ovid, Heroides 6-10, Metamorphoses 9; Seneca, Hercules Furens 177.
[386] Callimachus, Aetia, fragment 55.
[387] For this adventure being the first of Hercules' twelve labors, see Pindar, Isthmian 6, 46ff; Apollodorus, Library 2.74-76.; Theocritus, Idylls 25. 136ff; Diodorus, Library 4.11.3.
[388] Hesiod, Theogony, 327ff.
[389] Apollodorus, Library 2.74-76: a double-mouthed cave. Same detail in Diodorus, Library 4.11.3. Pausanias describes the location of the cave as being at a distance of 15 stades from Nemea (Pausanias, Description of Greece 2.15.2).
[390] Theocritus, Idylls 25.132.

country'[391] and during the reign of Mycenaean kings, such as Eurystheus, a natural hazard such as a monstrous beast that destroys cattle and flocks, posed a real menace to locals. The threat became even greater, since the size of the animal was not its prime characteristic of monstrosity: the lion was equipped with skin impervious to all kinds of weapons, so that no one could kill or merely wound it by sword, or arrow or spear. Hercules found out so himself, when he attacked the animal by arrows first,[392] and then by sword.[393]

Startled and confused, the animal ran back to its double-mouthed cave. Hercules followed it without fear and according to Apollodorus he blocked up one of the mouths of the cave so that the lion could not escape. Inside the cave he wrestled with the animal bare-handed, since no other force could subdue it. Hercules' uncanny strength helped choke the animal to death. 'He then draped it over his shoulders and brought it back to Cleonae'.[394]

Various details are found in different sources and they add to the complexity of the first adventure of Hercules. Before his encounter with the animal, Hercules arrived at an area called Cleonae. There he was received as a *xenos*, guest, by a local named Molorchus and connected with him via the sacred bonds of hospitality. Molorchus was a poor man who was about to offer sacrifice to the gods, when Hercules arrived. Hercules asked him to postpone his sacrificial offers for thirty days, hoping that by that time he would return a victor from his encounter with the lion. In that case, both he and the poor man would offer sacrifice to Zeus Soter, the Saviour; if Hercules would not return, then Molorchus would offer sacrifice to Hercules as a hero. As the days passed without a sign of Hercules, Molorchus prepared to sacrifice in his honor. It was then that Hercules arrived with the lion-skin and both he and the old man honored Zeus the Saviour.

Ptolemy Hephaestion (1st c. B.C.-1st c. A.D.) adds that the fight of Hercules with the lion did not come without a price, since the beast bit off one of Hercules' fingers, leaving him with nine for the rest of his life. He also refers to a tomb dedicated to the lost finger of Hercules, and adds an early explanation about the prominence of lion-statues at the tombs of exceptional men: 'other authors say that he lost his finger following a blow by a dart of a stingray and one can see at Sparta a stone lion erected on the tomb of the finger and which is the symbol of the power of the hero. It is since then that stone lions have likewise been erected on the tombs of other important people; other authors give different explications of the lion

---

[391] Theocritus, Idylls 25.135.
[392] Theocritus, Idylls 25.132
[393] Bacchylides, Fragment 13.
[394] Apollodorus, Library 2.74-76.

statues'.[395] The same source also claims that a strange serpent assisted Hercules in his struggle against the lion. It was a serpent born from the Earth (Gaea). Fed by Hercules, it had followed him to Thebes and stayed with him in a tent.[396]

The most detailed version of the struggle of Hercules with the lion is found in the 25th of Theocritus' *Idylls* (bucolic poetry of the 3rd c. B.C.), where the hero recounts his adventure to king Phyleus. According to his own words, the fight did not take place inside any cave, but out in the open. Hercules came to the land of Nemea prepared with his bow and a quiver full of arrows. It was mid-day when Hercules arrived at Nemea. Fear nested in the hearts of locals, who refrained even from daily tasks such as working in the fields with oxen, lest the lion attacked them. Hercules went deep into the grove of Zeus and lay in ambush for the lion. Hidden in the thick foliage of bushes, he waited until the lion appeared bloody from a fresh kill. Hercules shot an arrow at the lion, but its exceptional skin was not harmed. Then he struck it again right in the chest to no avail. He was about to strike for a third time when the lion spotted him. The beast arched his back and jumped on Hercules who was holding his arrows and folded cloak in one hand and menacingly held his club in the other. He smashed his club down the head of the charging animal, but the hardened olive-wood of his weapon simply broke on the lion's skull. Dazed by the blow, the animal was stunned with pain; it was then that Hercules advanced and seized it by the throat. He throttled it with stout hands coming behind it, to protect himself from its claws. Like a proper wrestler, Hercules pressed his knees hard against the animal's ribs and threw his weight on its back in order to throw it onto the ground. There he held it until its last breath was received by Hades.[397]

The interesting problem which comes next is also addressed by Theocritus. How do you skin an animal whose skin cannot be harmed by sword or knife? As Hercules put it, he had no knife or stone or other tool strong enough to cut the hide of the lion open; but a god – most probably Athena, his constant helper depicted regularly on his side in dozens of vase-paintings – put it in his mind to use the animals own claws: only the lion could hurt itself in this way. So Hercules slit the lion's hide with the animal's own claws. Utilizing this method, Hercules obtained the skin, which he used as 'a shield against the cut and thrust of the battle'.[398]

---

[395] Ptolemy Hephaestion, New History, book 2 (summary from Photius, Myriobiblon 190).
[396] Ptolemy Hephaestion, New History Book 2 (summary from Photius, Myriobiblon 190). Ptolemy refers to another source, Alexander of Myndos. Other writers who wrote about this story are mentioned by Hyginus ('Pisander and many other writers have written about this', Hyginus, Astronomica 2.24).
[397] Cf. Seneca, Hercules Furens, 83 ff; Statius, Thebaid 4.824ff; Nonnus, Dionysiaca 25.176ff
[398] Theocritus, Idylls 25. 132 ff. 132 ff. 132 ff.

When Hercules returned to Mycenae he presented this trophy to King Eurystheus as proof of his success. When Eurystheus saw the monstrous creature dangling from the shoulders of the hero, he was so scared that he ran and hid in one of the massive storage jars (*pithos*) found in Mycenaean archaeological sites. His cowardice was proven in that he ordered Hercules to announce his future reports on his adventures outside the gates of the city, via a herald named Copreus.[399] At least, the hero kept the trophy for himself. 'The skin of the lion he put about himself, and since he could cover his whole body with it because of its great size, he had in it a protection against the perils that were to follow'.[400]

From the 1st c. A.D. mostly Latin writers thought the Lion of Nemea was so exceptional that it became a constellation, that of Leo.[401] It must have been a very popular theme, not only in art of the archaic and classical period,[402] but also in theatre, since a lost play by Aeschylus is entitled *Leo* and it could be a satiric play referring to the killing of the Nemean Lion.

Phoenix (Φοῖνιξ)

The story of the Phoenix (Φοίνιξ),[403] the bird that dies in fire and is reborn from its own ashes, is placed at the leafy woods 'fringed by Ocean's farthest marge

---

[399] Diodorus, Library 4. 11; Theocritus, Idylls 25.
[400] Diodorus, Library 4.11.3.
[401] Seneca, Oedipus 38ff, Hercules Furens, 942ff; Hyginus, Astronomica 2.24.
[402] Besides the dozens of vases that depict the fight of Hercules with the lion, there are many statues of this theme. Pausanias describes a nude statue of a young Hercules shooting the lion, which was dedicated at Olympia (Pausanias, Description of Greece 5.27.7) and a painting of this labour found amongst the decoration of the temple of Zeus at Olympia (Pausanias, Description of Greece 5.11.5).
[403] The origin of the word is not clear. In Greek there is the adjective φοινός: crimson, deep red, which may allude to the colour of the bird, although no such description is found in the ancient sources. The Greeks also named Φοίνικες the people of Phoenicia, the Carthaginians, perhaps after their sunburned complexion. According to Liddell, Scott and Jones dictionary: φοῖνιξ, ῑκος, ὁ, purple or crimson, because the discovery and earliest use of this colour was ascribed to the Phoenicians, Il. 4.141, 6.219, Od.23.20. Ibid: V the fabulous bird phoenix, Hes. Fr.171.4, Antiph.175; from Arabia acc. to Hdt.2.73; but from India, Philostr. VA3.49: prov., φοίνικος ἔτη βιοῦν Luc.Herm.53 The phoenix is also found in the Bible's oldest book – the book of Job. Job 29:18 reads: 'Then I said: 'I shall die with my nest, and I shall multiply my days as the phoenix'.' However, this reading is debated, since it depends upon the translation of the Hebrew word chol, typically translated in one of three different ways: 1. Sand, 2. phoenix, as in the mythical bird, 3. palm tree. Each one of these meanings is correct and it would not cause problems to the translation of Job's words. The writer's personal opinion that the origin of the word for the bird Phoenix is Egyptian.

Detail from the 12th century Aberdeen Bestiary, featuring a phoenix

beyond the Indes and the East where Dawn's panting coursers first seek entrance'. It is described as *equal to the gods* and it has no need of drink or food. It is fed by sunbeams and drinks the sprays of the sea.[404]

According to all of our sources, from Hesiod to Claudian, there are no parents to this strange bird. Parented by no previous creator other than itself, every one thousand years, it grows weary and senses its death. Then it gathers up branches and dry herbs, builds a pyre which 'shall be at once his tomb and his cradle'.[405]

> Never was this bird conceived nor springs it from any mortal seed, itself is alike its own father and son, and with none to recreate it, it renews its outworn limbs with a rejuvenation of death, and at each decease wins a fresh lease of life.[406]

The bird is thus the creator and perpetuator of its own kind and thus remains today the eternal symbol of the power to overcome difficulties and generate proverbial phrases such 'to be reborn from one's own ashes'.

The Phoenix is impressive. Claudian describes him as a creature with fiery flashing eyes, a flaming aureole around its head, bright crest, purple legs and blue wings dappled with rich gold.[407]

The life span of the Phoenix is one thousand years. 'For when a thousand summers have passed far away, a thousand winters gone by, a thousand springs in

---

[404] Claudian, XVII, 1-22 (transl. by Maurice Platnauer)
[405] Herodotus 2.73, Ovid Metamorphoses 15.385, Apollonius of Tyana 1.38, Claudian Phoenix, XVII, 36.
[406] Claudian, XVII, 23-25.
[407] Claudian, XVII, 20-22.

their course given to the husbandmen that shade of which autumn robbed them, then at last, fordone by the number of its years, it falls a victim to the burden of age'.[408]

In Jewish tradition there are stories about the Milcham, a beautiful bird that lived in the Garden of Eden. Eve persuaded all the animals to eat from the tree of Knowledge, but the Milcham refused. For this it was rewarded with immortality. Every thousand years it was consumed by fire and from a single egg that it left behind a new Milcham was born. For the Egyptians the Phoenix-like bird is called Bennu and it was associated with the god of creation, Atum, later with Ra and finally with Osiris. According to the Egyptians, the Phoenix arrived at Heliopolis, at the *Temple of the Phoenix* every 1460 years, signifying the end of the cycle of Soth, or cycle of Sirius (the constellation) known as 'Ideal New Year'. In Hindu tradition it is called Carunda and it is associated with the Avatar of Vishnu, Ram the Sun God. The Chinese believe that the Phoenix lives in the South, which is associated with Fire.

Hippalectryon (Ιππαλεκτρυών)

On a great number of vase paintings dating around the 6th c. B.C., we come across a strange animal form: a being with the front part of a horse and the back of a large bird or a rooster. This is the Hippalectryon, the name signifying without a doubt the constituents of this unusual hybrid, since *hippos* means horse and *alectryon* means rooster.[409] There are no surviving mythological traditions related to the Hippalectryon, with some exceptional references to it by 5th c. B.C. writers, such as Aristophanes – something that probably makes sense, if one considers the potentially comic look of this monster.

It makes an early appearance as a popular theme in plastic art and paintings. The oldest finding we possess is dated around the 9th c. B.C. at Cnossus, Crete. Around the 6th c. B.C., it seems that the form has received a commonly consistent shape, which often decorates coins from that period, but mostly black-figure Attic vase paintings: the front part with the front legs of a horse and the back of what seems to be either a rooster with its characteristic feathers of the tail or a large bird. A great number of the vase-paintings from the 6th c. B.C. depict a young warrior riding it.[410]

---

[408] Claudian, XVII, 36-38.
[409] Hippos (ἵππος): horse and alectryon (ἀλεκτρυών): rooster.
[410] See, for example, the beautiful siana cup , attributed to the Gryps painter, circa 56-550 B.C. now kept at Harvard University Art Museums, Cambridge Massachusetts, U.S.A., and the Attic black-figure Kylix attributed to the Xenocles painter, circa 550 B.C., now kept at the

Man riding hippalektryon. Interior of an Attic black-figure lip cup, 540–530 BC.

Literary sources do not shed more light on the appearance of the Hippalectryon. The only actual description we have comes from Aristophanes' *Peace*, suggesting a rather yellowish or light brown color of the feathers:

> *and then I grow fat*
> *during summer,*
> *better than looking at a god-hated general*
> *with three plumes and crimson cloak*
> *which he claims that it is painted with dye from Sardis;*
> *if, however, somewhere he has to fight with this cloak,*
> *then he is painted with pale dye from Cyzicus;*
> *and he is first to flee from the battle, like a blond hippalectryon,*
> *shaking his plumes.*[411]

University Museums, University of Mississippi, Oxford Mississippi, U.S.A. An interesting black-figure kylix, attributed to the painter of the Vatican Horseman, from around 530-520 B.C. (Tampa Museum of Art, Tampa, Florida, U.S.A.) shows a menacing, fully armed warrior standing on the back of a bridled Hippalectryon.

[411] Aristophanes, Peace 1170-8 (transl. Syropoulos).

Perhaps the strange animal gained literary fame during the 5th c. B.C. and emerged from anonymity and low status to something more popular. This is what we infer from the derogatory comment of Aristophanes, regarding a certain general Dieitrephes, who rose to fame although he did not seem to possess any substantial qualities:

So, is it not worth anything, for someone to be winged?
Just like Dieitrephes, possessing merely wicker-feathers,
he was elected Phylarchos (leader of his Tribe), *and then hipparchos,*
then from being nobody, he is now famous and now he is a blond hippalectryon.[412]

Despite its popularity on vase-paintings, it seems that Aristophanes did not consider it a very heroic symbol; in fact, the confusing form of the hippalectryon seems to be used as mockery for Aeschylus' hyper-sophisticated vocabulary and his love for word-combination. In his *Frogs,* the god of theatre, Dionysus, descends to the underworld to fetch back to life a worthwhile poet, in order to advise the Athenians how to best rule their city. A contest between the two dead poets, Euripides and Aeschylus, presents us with the world's first extended literary criticism and potential undermining of Aeschylus' theatrical language.

Dionysus: By Gods! Many long nights I stayed awake,
trying to figure out which bird was the blond hippalectryon.
Aeschylus: It was a figure engraved on ships, you ignoramus!
Dionysus: And I thought that it was Eryxes, the son of Philoxenus.
Euripides: And so, you had to make a hippalectryon in your tragedies?
Aeschylus: And you, god-hated man, what where the things you made?
Euripides: Not hippalectryons, by Zeus, and no goat-stags (τραγέλαφους), *like you did.*[413]

A comment on Aeschylus' lost play *Myrmidones,* describes how the figure of a Hippalectryon seems to be attached to the ship of the Marathon-battle hero, Cynegeirus (brother of Aeschylus).[414] The fact that the peculiar creature was depicted on war-ships and on shields might indicate some kind of apotropaic use, just like the popular head of Medusa on shields and breast-plates: a picture as odd as that of Hippalectryon might confuse – even frighten – the enemy; at worst, it would cause laughter.

---

[412] Aristophanes, Birds 797-800.
[413] Aristophanes, Frogs 931-8.
[414] Aeschylus, fragment 61, Myrmidones (from Scholiast on Aristophanes' Peace 1177).

According to the Greek grammarian Hesychius,[415] there is a confusion regarding the form of this monster, and no literary sources before Aeschylus are mentioned by him (Aesch. fr. 134).[416]

Hesychius claims that the animal is either a big rooster, or a kind of griffin, or, according to some, a vulture.

---

[415] Hesychius of Alexandria (Greek: Ἡσύχιος ὁ Ἀλεξανδρεύς), a Greek grammarian who probably flourished probably at the end of the 5th century AD, compiled (probably absorbing the work of earlier lexicographers) the richest lexicon of unusual and obscure Greek words that has survived (in a single 15th-century manuscript). The work, titled 'Alphabetical Collection of All Words' (Συναγωγὴ Πασῶν Λέξεων κατὰ Στοιχεῖον), includes more than 50.000 entries, a copious list of peculiar words, forms and phrases, with an explanation of their meaning, and often with a reference to the author who used them or to the district of Greece where they were current.

[416] Hesychius, Lexicon. Alphabetical letter iota entry 780,1-3.

Chapter 5
Ghosts and Daemons

No matter how big or voracious, human-like or bestial, hybrid or simply endowed with extraordinary features, the monstrous forms that we have encountered so far share one common characteristic: they are tangible. It might be difficult to overcome them, yet not impossible; given the right lineage, especially if this is divine, or the right weapons, especially if they are given by the gods, or simply by cunning and strength, all monsters can be confronted. What do you do, though, with the ones you cannot face, simply because they literally cannot be materialized, or seen? The ultimate transgression of the ordinary is to be found outside the boundaries of the known world. There is another world, more fearsome because it is more or less uncharted. A world beyond human comprehension and physical existence. It is the realm of Ghosts and Daemons.

Eidola (Εἴδωλα)

The idea of a non-tangible afterlife existence which can communicate with the world of the living is recorded since the time of Homer. The oldest recorded encounter of the living with the dead is found in the *Iliad*. In book 23 dead Patroclus appears to his best friend Achilles, in the form of an apparition, a non-tangible ghost.

> *And there appeared to him the ghost of unhappy Patroklos*   65
> *all in his likeness for stature, and the lovely eyes, and voice,*
> *and wore such clothing as Patroklos had worn on his body.*
> *The ghost came and stood over his head and spoke a word to him:*
> *'You sleep, Achilleus; you have forgotten me; but you were not*
> *careless of me when I lived, but only in death. Bury me*   70
> *as quickly as may be, let me pass through the gates of Hades.*
> *The souls, the images of dead men, hold me at a distance,*
> *and will not let me cross the river and mingle among them,*
> *but I wander as I am by Hades' house of the wide gates.* [417]

Achilles protests to Patroclus' accusations of not taking care of the funerary rites fast enough, so that the soul can be received by the other souls of the dead

---
[417] Homer, Iliad, 23. 65-74 (transl. Lattimore).

in the House of Hades. He asks Patroclus to come and embrace him, like before, but when he extends his arms and tries to hug his friend, the spirit of Patroclus vanishes 'as in vapor, gibbering and whining into the earth':

> So he spoke, and with his own arms reached for him, but could not
> take him, but the spirit went underground, like vapor,   100
> with a thin cry, and Achilleus started awake, staring,
> and drove his hands together, and spoke, and his words were sorrowful:
> 'Oh, wonder! Even in the house of Hades there is left something,
> a soul and an image, but there is no real heart of life in it.
> For all night long the phantom of unhappy Patroklos   105
> stood over me in lamentation and mourning, and the likeness
> to him was wonderful, and it told me each thing I should do'.[418]

In this passage we have the most ancient use of the word *eidolon* (idol, reflection) in association with the souls of the dead, which are like a reflection of the living.[419] It is found once more in the *Iliad* (Book, 23, line 104) and another six times in the *Odyssey*.[420] Especially in the *Odyssey* it is interesting to draw attention to book 24, where after the killing of the suitors by Odysseus, Eumaius and Telemachus, Theoclymenus sees the doorway of the court filled with the *eidola* of the dead.[421]

In general, though, the eidola of the dead are not malignant or vicious. Complicated – perhaps contradictory and not very consistent[422] – ideas about this kind of existence are found in the famous *Nekyia*, the eleventh book of the *Odyssey* (from the word *nekys*: dead), the book which describes the descent of Odysseus into the underworld, in order to communicate with the souls of the dead, especially the soul of the seer Teiresias, and gain valuable information about how to return home. The dead cannot communicate with the living, unless they have drunk from the blood of the butchered black ram that Odysseus sacrificed for them. This has nothing to do with the 'modern' notions of blood-thirsty vampires and zombies of

---

[418] Homer, Iliad, 23. 99-107 (transl. Lattimore).
[419] Homer, Iliad 23. 72:) tÁlš me e‡rgousi yucaˆ e‡dwla kamÒntwn.
[420] Homer, Odyssey 11. 83, 213, 476, 602; 20. 355; 24. 14.
[421] Homer, Odyssey, 24. 14. Cf. Barasch (2005) 13-28.
[422] For example, the souls that Odysseus encounters are definitely non-tangible and it is a very touching description of the scene where he tries to embrace his mother, only to realize that she is as if made of vapour. The bodies of the dead have no substance, no matter. Nevertheless, he scares the thirsty souls away from the blood of the sacrificed ram, by wielding a bronze sword, as he waits for the soul of Teiresias to be the first to drink from the blood. Unless bronze has some magical averting powers – something no where stated – this scene does not make sense.

modern literature and cinematography. The dead are distinguished from the living because of the absence of blood. It is this single feature that turns them into *eidola*, reflections of the living. Only once they put blood back into their forms, can they regain consciousness and communicate with the living. Of course, this happens only in the underworld. The ghost of Patroclus has no need of blood, in order to communicate with the living Achilles. One might argue that Patroclus appeared to Achilles in a dream; or that outside the realm of Hades, there is no need for blood consumption; or simply, no consistency should be demanded from a genre that probably comprised of many different times and traditions.

Certainly things have changed dramatically on the dramatic stage of 5th c. B.C. Athens. In the only recorded necromantic scene performed in front of the eyes of the mesmerized audience of Aeschylus' *Persians* (472 B.C.), the ghost of Darius, evoked with an elaborate ritual of libations, shouts and dances, appears in front of his subjects and his wife, and needs no blood to communicate with them. The libations of milk, honey and wine suffice to bring him to the surface and he asks for nothing more, before he bestows his long-gathered wisdom upon them.[423] A lot has been transformed since the times of Homer.

More information about ghosts comes from the Athenian stage of the 5th c. B.C. In the *Phoenician Women* of Euripides, Oedipus likens himself to an *eidolon* made of air, or *nekyn* (dead) or winged dream from dark rooms underneath the earth, from where his daughter has called him out.[424] Also, in the *Alcestis* of Euripides, when Admetus is presented with his dead wife whom Hercules has just brought back from death, he asks the great hero whether he thinks that she is a ghost (φάσμα) from Hades.[425] Again, we are presented with the same notion: ghosts may still resemble the living in form, but they are nothing more than their shadowy reflections.[426]

Communication with the dead is not uncommon. Specialized shrines dedicated to this kind of communication are found in the vicinity of Greece throughout the classical period, the so-called *nekyomanteia,* oracles of the dead.[427]

---

[423] As argued by Συρόπουλος (2012) 96-105 the dead king, just like other ghosts that are evoked in order to offer advice to the living, is not able to tell the future. He only gives enlightened advice based on his experience and wisdom that he gathered while alive. The ghosts of people are not endowed with supernatural powers or predictive abilities.
[424] Euripides, Phoenician Women 1539-1545. Cf. Συρόπουλος (2012) 86.
[425] Euripides, Alcestis 1127.
[426] For detailed analysis of cases of ghosts appearing on the dramatic stage of classical Athens, see Aguirre Castro (2006) 107-120.
[427] Already in the 5th c. B.C. there were five known nekyomanteia (places where one can consult the dead) or psychopompeia (places where one could call the dead to manifest themselves, in order to offer advice or information) in Greece. The most famous one was the nekyomanteion of Acheron in Thesprotia (Herodotus 5.92) and then there was the

Hermes guides a dead soul to Hades, attributed to the Sabouroff Painter, c. 450 BC.

In the 5th c B.C. communication between the world of the dead and the world of the living was an undeniable fact, commonly accepted in Greece. Some of the parameters of this kind of communication are recorded in the story of the tyrant of Corinth Periander and his wife, Melissa.[428] 'Periander, who had lost his queen, Melissa, sent representatives to the oracle of the dead, in order to consult her over a misplaced item. She refused to help him, because, as she said, she was cold and naked, since the clothes with which she was buried had not been burnt properly, so they were of no use. In order to convince Periander, Melissa sent him the message that *he had put his bread in a cold oven.* Periander got upset, because he had had intercourse with his wife's corpse. In order to redeem himself, Periander ordered his soldiers to strip off all the women of Corinth and burn their clothes in a pit. Only then Melissa revealed to him the location of the item he was looking for'.[429]

Ghosts, however can be malignant. Not in the classical period, but as the world evolves and becomes more complicated, and, most probably, as new ideas from the East pervade religious beliefs and concepts of the afterlife for the Greeks, the world of the dead becomes more alienated from the world of the living, and definitely more scary. The once simple reflections, or *eidola* of the dead, now become dreadful tormentors of the living.

---

nekyomanteia in Heracleia of Pontus, in Asia Minor (Plutarch, Cimon 6), in Phygaleia (Arcadia), in Hermione (Argolis) and in Cyme, at the lake Avernus (Italy) described by Strabo (C. 244-6 and Ephorus FGH70,F134a). The nekyomanteion of Acheron is mentioned in the Odyssey (Homer, Odyssey 11.488ff). Cf. Συρόπουλος (2012) 87-88.

[428] Herodotus, 5. 92.
[429] Συρόπουλος (2012) 89.

The new-age eidola are entities from a world beyond ours. They are not specified as souls of the dead, but simply as ghosts able to possess the living. Two of the most notable cases of such incidents are described by a Neopythagorean philosopher of the 1st c. A.D., Apollonius of Tyana. (Ἀπολλώνιος ὁ Τυανεύς; c. 15 – c. 100 A.D).[430] Although not much is certain about his life and teaching, the main doctrines of his work survived thanks to Philostratus (Lucius Flavius Philostratus or Φλάβιος Φιλόστρατος), a Greek sophist and biographer who lived between 170/172-247/250 A.D.[431] More than a quarter of his work *Life of Apollonius* is devoted to a journey of Apollonius to India, where he met a native named Datis, who became his lifelong companion.[432] There he describes two cases of possession by spirits. The word used is the archaic and classical period *eidolon*, but the characteristics of these entities resemble nothing of the *eidola* of the Homeric world. The first case is about a sixteen-year-old boy of India possessed by an eidolon, a Daemon that was a mocker and liar. It is the spirit of a man who 'wears her son as a mask', the mother of the boy explains, adding that her son was possessed by this spirit because he was good-looking and the daemon was 'amorous of him'. The daemon/eidolon had the power to fully control the body of its hapless victim and threatened the mother that he might drive the boy to jump off a cliff and be killed, lest she took measures against the possession:

And he [a messenger to the sages of India] brought forward a poor woman who interceded on behalf of her child, who was, she said, a boy of sixteen years of age,

---

[430] Apollonius was Greek, born at Tyana, in the Roman province of Cappadocia in Asia Minor. Considering that he lived around the same time as Jesus, it is not surprising that many writers of that period compared the two of them. For his life, see Dzielska (1986). The classic work that compares Jesus and Apollonius as individuals who shared similar hero stories is that of Joseph Campbell, The Hero with a Thousand Faces, 1949. Also, Robert Price (2011) p. 20, who claims that both individuals fit the mythic hero archetype.

[431] The biographical Life of Apollonius of Tyana was written at the request of empress Julia Domna, wife of Septimus Severus and mother of Caracalla. She did not live to see the book completed. She died in 217 A.D. and the work of Philostratus was completed around the 220s or 230s A.D. This work has not survived entire, but excerpts from it are found in the work of Eusebius. Philostratus himself claims to have in his possession the diary of Damis, a companion of Apollonius, although many scholars believe that this diary was an invention of Philostratus. Cf. Bowie (2005).

[432] Two and a half of his eight books of his Life of Apollonius (1.19-3.58) are devoted to this journey. His visit to India could be a fabrication of Philostratus, since many details described in this work seem incompatible with known facts. However, modern scholarship does not rule out the possibility of an actual journey to India. Cf. Graham Anderson, (1986) pp. 199-215; Flinterman (1995) pp. 86-87, 101-106.

but had been, for two years, possessed by an Eidolon (phantom). Now the character of the Daemon was that of a mocker and a liar. Here one of the sages asked, why she said this, and she replied : 'This child of mine is extremely good-looking, and therefore the Daemon is amorous of him and will not allow him to retain his reason, nor will he permit him to go to school, or to learn archery, nor even to remain at home, but drives him out into desert places and the boy does not even retain his own voice, but speaks in a deep hollow tone, as men do; and he looks at you with other eyes rather than with his own. As for myself I weep over all this and I tear my cheeks, and I rebuke my son so far as I well may; but he does not know me;. [...] only the Daemon discovered himself using my child as a mask, and what he told me was this, that he was the ghost of a man, who fell long ago in battle, but that at death he was passionately attached to his wife. Now he had been dead for only three days when his wife insulted their union by marrying another man, and the consequence was that he had come to detest the love of women, and had transferred himself wholly into this boy. But he promised, if I would only not denounce him, to endow the child with many noble blessings. As for myself, I was influenced by these promises; but he has put me off and off for such a long time now, that he has got sole control of my household, yet has no honest or true intentions.'

Here the sage asked afresh, if the boy was at hand; and she said not, for, although she had done all she could to get him to come with her, the Daemon had threatened her with steep places and precipices and declared that he would kill her son, 'in case', she added, 'I haled him hither for trial.'

'Take courage,' said the sage, 'for he will not slay him when he has read this.' And so saying he drew a letter out of his bosom and gave it to the woman; and the letter, it appears, was addressed to the ghost and contained threats of an alarming kind.[433]

As it seems, Apollonius, described as a sage, possesses magical, apotropaic writings that have the power to exorcise the eidolon away from the sufferer. This becomes clearer in the second case of possession that Philostratus describes.

The person possessed seems to live an ordinary existence amongst the rest of the community, unaware of his predicament, which is obviously not immediately perceived by the rest of the community. Philostratus now describes a case of possession by an eidolon this time in Athens, where a young man's insolent behavior leads Apollonius to the conclusion that he is possessed. The body of the young man is merely the mouthpiece of the eidolon. However, the powers of the daemon extend beyond the physical abilities of the person who carries him. The spirit has the power of telekinesis, i.e. moving objects from afar, just by pointing the finger of the body that carried him at them. Apollonius' powers seem to be very much known and acknowledged by the

---

[433] Philostratus, Life of Apollonius of Tyana, 3.38 (transl. Conybeare).

eidola, since it takes just one look of the sophist in the eyes of the possessed boy, to scare the daemon inside him so much, that he cries out in fear and rage and promises not only to leave the boy, but also to never haunt anyone again.

> *Now while he was discussing the question of libations, there chanced to be present in his audience a young dandy who bore so evil a reputation for licentiousness, that his conduct had been the subject of coarse street-corner songs. His home was Corcyra and he traced his pedigree to Alcinous, the Phaeacian who entertained Odysseus. Apollonius then was talking about libations, and was urging them not to drink out of a particular cup, but to reserve it for the gods, without ever touching it drinking out of it. But when he also urged them to have handles on the cup, and to pour the libation over the handle, because that is the part of the cup at which men are least likely to drink, the young burst out into loud and coarse laughter, and quite drowned his voice. Then Apollonius looked up at him and said: 'It is not yourself that perpetrates this insult, but the demon, who drives you on without your knowing it'. And in fact the youth was, without knowing it, possessed by a devil; for he would laugh at things that no one else laughed at, and then he would fall to weeping for no reason at all, and he would talk and sing to himself. Now most people thought that it was the boisterous humour of youth which led him into such excesses; but he was really the mouth-piece of a devil, though it only seemed a drunken frolic in which on that occasion he was indulging. Now when Apollonius gazed on him, the demon in him began to utter cries of fear and rage, such as one hears from people who are being branded or racked; and the demon swore that he would leave the young man alone and never take possession of any many again. But Apollonius addressed him with anger, as a master might a shifty, rascally and shameless slave and so on, and he ordered him to quit the young man and show by a visible sign that he had done so. 'I will throw down yonder statue', said the devil and pointed to one of the images which was in the king's portico, for there it was that the scene took place. But when the statue began by moving gently, and then fell down, it would defy anyone to describe the hubbub which arose thereat and the way the clapped their hands with wonder. But the young man rubbed his eyes as if he had just woken up, and he looked towards the rays of the sun, and won the consideration of all, who now had turned their attention to him; for he no longer showed himself licentious, nor did he stare madly about, but he had returned to his own self, as thoroughly as if he had been treated with drugs; and he gave up his dainty dress and summery garments and the rest of his sybaritic way of life, and he fell in love with the austerity of philosophers and donned their cloak, and stripping off his old self modeled his life in the future upon that of Apollonius.*[434]

---

[434] Philostratus, Life of Apollonius of Tyana, 4. 20 ff. Cf. Erickson (1980) 122.

It is noteworthy that after his exorcism the young man, whose conduct was previously insolent and licentious, turned to a more 'righteous' way of life, i.e. the life ordered by the doctrines of the enlightened sophist Apollonius. Rationalization of such exorcisms and possessions put aside, stories about eidola and their powers were regarded seriously by orators like Eusebius in the 4th c. A.D., who is also responsible for some of our knowledge about the life and deeds of Apollonius.

> *Apollonios as they say, drives out one Daemon with the help of another. The first of the Daemones is expelled from an incorrigible youth, while the second disguises itself by assuming the form of a woman: and the latter our clever author calls by no other names than those of Empousa and Lamia.*[435]

The names of more 'traditional' ghosts, like the Empousa and the Lamia are mentioned as part of the exorcism and will both be presented shortly. In any case, they add to the powers of Apollonius the authority of the supernatural, since they seem to create a whole system of classification of entities that can and should be dealt with, since they are definitely malignant.

> *Morevover, the soul of Achilles should not have been lingering about his own monument, quitting the Islands of the Blest and the places of repose, as people would probably say. In this case too it was surely a demon that appeared to Apollonius and in whose presence he found himself? Then again the licentious youth was clearly the victim of an indwelling demon; and both it and the Empousa and the Lamia, which is said to have played off its mad pranks on Menippus, were probably driven out by him with the help of a more important demon.*[436]

Ghosts and apparitions continued to fascinate the minds of people in Greece. The possibility of an afterlife from which one could return, was intriguing. Such is the case of Philinion, a girl from Macedonia who found her way back from the realm of Hades to enjoy the pleasures of married life, as she had died unwed. The story is recorded by a 2nd c. A.D. writer named Phlegon of Tralles, who reported a story that came from 4th c. B.C. Macedonia. According to Phlegon's narrative Phillinion died young and without having experienced the pleasures of marriage. This is obviously the reason behind her return from the dead. Phillinion is said

---

[435] Eusebius, Treatise of Eusebius against Hierocles, 26 (transl. Jones).
[436] Euseubius, Treatise of Eusebius against Hierocles, 31. Transl. Erickson (1980) 123. On the same page Erickson writes: 'it is interesting that Eusebius, reflecting the Christian viewpoint, does not deny the reality of the exorcisms or even the miracles, but attributes his success to the complicity of demons'.

GHOSTS AND DAEMONS 117

Lekythos from the Achilles Painter; c 440 BC. The symbol over the figure on the right marks him as a dead soul.

to have been visiting a certain youth named Machates, with whom she started a secret erotic relationship. Unlike the apparitions described in the Homeric epics, this ghost seems to have possessed proper substance – at least this is what we infer from the fact that young Machates was not alarmed by anything unusual about his nightly visitor. Demostratus and Charito, her parents, however, were shocked when they found out about their daughter's return from the grave. Although there seems to be nothing sinister about these night visits to the young man, the community reacted in a way that reveals grave fear. The final burning of Phillinion's body seems to have put a stop to her ability to transgress the limits between the world of the living and the afterlife. From Hansen's translation, I quote:

> *The nurse went to the door of the guest room, and in the light of the burning lamp she saw the girl [Phillinion who died and had been entombed many months before] sitting beside Makhates. Because of the extraordinary nature of the sight, she did not wait there any longer but ran to the girl's mother screaming, 'Kharito! Demostratos!' She said they should get up and come with her to their daughter, who was alive and by some divine will was with the guest in the guest room.*
> *When Kharito heard this astonishing report, the immensity of the message and the nurse's excitement made her frightened and faint. But after a short time the memory of her daughter came to her, and she began to weep; in the end she accused the old woman of being mad and told her to leave her presence immediately. But the nurse replied boldly and reproachfully that she herself was rational and sound of mind, unlike her mistress, who was reluctant to see her own daughter. With some hesitation Kharito went to the door of the guest room, partly coerced by the nurse and partly wanting to know what really had happened. Since considerable time--about two hours--had now passed since the nurse's original message, it was somewhat late when Kharito went to the door and the occupants were already asleep. She peered in and though she recognised her daughter's clothes and features, but inasmuch as she could not determine the truth of the matter she decided to do nothing further that night. She planned to get up in the morning and confront the girl, or if she should be too late for that she intended to question Makhates thoroughly about everything. He would not, she thought, lie if asked about so important a matter. And so she said nothing and left.*
> *At dawn, however, it turned out that by divine will or chance the girl had left unnoticed. When Kharito came to the room she was upset with the young man because of the girl's departure. She asked him to relate everything to her from the beginning, telling the truth and concealing nothing.*
> *The youth was anxious and confused at first, but hesitantly revealed the girl's name was Philinnion. He told how her visits began, how great her desire for him was, and that she said she came to him without her parents' knowledge. Wishing to make the*

matter credible he opened his coffer and took out the items the girl had left behind-- the golden ring he had obtained from her and the breast-band she had left the night before.
When Kharito saw this evidence she uttered a cry, tore her clothes, cast her headdress from her head and fell to the ground, throwing herself upon the tokens and beginning her grief anew. As the guest observed what was happening, how all were grieving and wailing as if they were about to lay the girl into her grave, he became upset and called upon them to stop, promising to show them the girl if she came again. Kharito accepted this and bade him carefully keep his promise to her.
Night came on and now it was the hour when Philinnion was accustomed to come to him. The household kept watch wanting to know of her arrival. She entered at the usual time and sat down on the bed. Makhates pretended that nothing was wrong, since he wished to investigate the whole incredible matter to find out if the girl he was consorting with, who took care to come to him at the same hour, was actually dead. As she ate and drank with him, he simply could not believe what the others had told him, and he supposed that some grave-robbers had dug into the tomb and sold the clothes and gold to her father. But in his wish to learn exactly what the case was, he secretly sent his slaves to summon Demostratos and Kharito.
They came quickly. When they first saw her they were speechless and panic-stricken by the amazing sight, but after that they cried aloud and embraced their daughter. Then Philinnion said to them : `Mother and father, how unfairly you have grudged my being with the guest for three days in my father's house, since I have caused no one any pain. For this reason, on account of your meddling, you shall grieve all over again, and I shall return to the place appointed for me. For it was not without divine will that I came here.' Immediately upon speaking these words she was dead, and her body lay stretched visibly on the bed. Her father and mother threw themselves upon her, and there was much confusion and wailing in the house because of the calamity. The misfortune was unbearable and the sight incredible.
The event was quickly heard through the city and was reported to me. Accordingly, during the night I kept in check the crowds that gathered at the house, since, with news like this going from mouth to mouth, I wanted to make sure there would be no trouble.
By early dawn the town assembly was full. After the particulars had been explained, it was decided that we should first go to the tomb, open it, and see whether the body lay on its bier or whether we would find the place empty. A half-year had not yet passed since the death of the girl. When we opened the chamber into which all deceased members of the family were placed, we saw bodies lying on biers, or bones in the case of those who had died long ago, but on the bier onto which Philinnion had been placed we found only the iron ring that belonged to the guest and the gilded wine cup, objects that she had obtained from Makhates on the first day.

> Astonished and frightened, we proceeded immediately to Demostratos's house to see if the corpse was truly to be seen in the guest room. After we saw the dead girl lying there on the ground, we gathered at the place of assembly, since the events were serious and incredible.
> There was considerable confusion in the assembly and almost no one was able to form a judgment on the events. The first to stand up was Hyllos, who is considered to be not only the best seer among us but also a fine augur; in general, he has shown remarkable perception in his craft. He said we should burn the girl outside the boundaries of the city, since nothing would be gained by burying her in the ground within its boundaries, and perform an apotropaic sacrifice to Hermes Khthonios (of the Underworld) and the Eumenides [Erinyes]. Then he prescribed that everyone purify himself completely, cleanse the temples and perform all the customary rites to the Khthonion (Underworld) Gods. He spoke to me also in private about the king and the events, telling me to sacrifice to Hermes, Zeus Xenios and Ares, and to perform these rites with care. When he had made this known to us, we undertook to do what he had prescribed. Makhates, the guest whom the ghost had visited, became despondent and killed himself.
> If you decide to write about this to the king, send word to me also in order that I may dispatch to you one of the persons who examined the affair in detail. Farewell.[437]

The story seems to have been well known during the 5th c. A.D., since it is recorded by another writer, the neo-platonic philosopher Proclus, who names Hipparchus and Arrhidaeus as his sources. In his version, the girl was married to a certain Craterus, but she died young, six months after her marriage. Then, just like described in the narrative of Phlegon, she returned to consort with Machates.

> Persons who died and returned to life . . . The case par excellence is Philinnion, during the reign of Philip [of Makedon]. The daughter of the Amphipolitans Demostratos and Charito, she died as a newly-wed. Her husband had been Krateros. In the sixth month after her death she returned to life and for many nights in a row secretly consorted with a young man, Makhates, because of her love for him. He had come to Demostratos from his native city of Pella. She was detected and died again after proclaiming that what she had done was done in accord with the will of the Khthonioi (Underworld) Gods. Her corpse was seen by everyone as it lay in state in her father's house. In their disbelief at what had happened the members of her family went to the place that had earlier received her body, dug the place up and found it to be empty. The events are described in

---

[437] Phlegon of Tralles, Book of Marvels 2. 1 (transl. Hansen).

a number of letters, some written by Hipparchos and some written by Arrhidaios (who was in charge of Amphipolis) to Philip.[438]

Proclus knows more cases of people who returned from the dead. In the same work he mentions first of all, Rufus of Thessaloniki of Macedonia:

Rufus from Philippi of Macedonia, who was fortunate enough to have been a high priest at Thessalonice; after he died he was resurrected three years later and having returned from the afterlife he said that he was sent back from the chthonic gods, in order to complete the tasks that he had promised to undertake for the benefit of the people, and that he would live until these had been completed.[439]

Other people who returned from the world of the dead are mentioned in Proclus' work, such as Polycritus of Aetolia, who died and returned to life nine months after his death, only to attend the assembly of the Aetolians and offer his advice, as he had happened to be one of the foremost citizens of the community.[440] It is worth noticing that nothing evil is found in this story; just like in the case of the resurrection of Darius in the *Persians* of Aeschylus, the ghost of a wise man of a previous generation, returns to life in order to offer his precious wisdom for the benefit of the community.[441] Fascination with knowledge from the life beyond, not previous experience, is obvious in the case of Eurynous; he was resurrected fifteen days after his burial and 'he said that he saw and heard many wondrous things under the earth, but he was commanded to keep all of them secret. And he lived for a long time and he appeared to be younger just after his resurrection than before'.[442]

From the above non-systematic and often conflicting information about the existence of an afterlife and the parameters for the possibility of transgressing boundaries between life and death, only one conclusion can be drawn with certainty: if there is Truth and Wisdom in the afterlife, it is not to be shared with the living. The dead can only return to demand from the living appropriate farewell rituals, so that they can move on (the case of Patroclus in the *Iliad*), to offer knowledge that was theirs before they died (Darius in the *Persians* or Eurynomous in the work of Proclus), or simply to steal moments of mundane pleasure that they

---
[438] Proclus, In Platonis Rem Publicam Commentarii, 2.115.2-2.116.18 (transl. Hansen).
[439] Proclus, In Platonis Rem Publicam Commentarii 2.115.24-2.116.2 (transl. Syropoulos).
[440] Proclus, In Platonis Rem Publicam Commentarii 2.115.7-2.115.-15.
[441] Proclus mentions his sources for this case: Clearchus, Naumachius of Epirus, Hieron of Ephesus and other historians (Proclus, In Platonis Rem Publicam Commentarii, 2.115.7-2.115.-15(.
[442] Proclus, In Platonis Rem Publicam Commentarii, 2.115.19-2.115.23.

did not have the chance to experience (the case of Phillinion). One might be a better person, after having experienced death, like Eurynous; but whether this happens because what he experienced in the afterlife was reward or punishment for his previous life-style, never becomes clear.

Empousa (Ἔμπουσα)

Apparitions from the world beyond are scary when they are invisible, like the eidola of the dead; they can be equally frightening when they are not of particular shape, but rather shift forms at will. The absence of matter, as in the case of eidola, makes them incomprehensible; form-changing is a power that the gods possess, in general. Gods can take up any shape or form they desire. Zeus, for instance, has taken up so many different forms, that it would take a whole book just to present his manifold manifestations. However, they are all transformations into shapes and life-forms that are immediately recognized and familiar to humans. The same can be said for Athena, who transformed herself so often in the *Odyssey*, or for the various transformations of Thetis, in order to escape Peleus, or so many other gods and goddesses. However, the known shapes can curdle the blood in the veins of the living when they are faced with the terrible Empousa;[443] and it becomes worse when she combines known features in one monstrous compilation.

Empousa (Ἔμπουσα, found frequently in the plural Ἔμπουσαι) was a female daemon of the underworld. She is an entity that feeds upon human flesh, like her sisters Lamia (Λάμια) and Mormolyce (Μορμώ, Μορμολύκη).

This strange appearance is owed to Aristophanes' *Frogs*, a play about the descent of Dionysus and his slave, Xanthias, in the underworld. After they have crossed the lake of Acheron, they come across an Empousa, guarding the entrance to Hades:

> Xanthias : By Zeus, I hear some loud noise   285
> Dionysus: Where, where is it?
> Xanthias:Behind us.
> Dionysus: Then, come behind me.
> Xanthias: But, it is in front of us now.
> Dionysus: Then, stand in front of me.
> Xanthias: And there, by Zeus, I see now a great beast.

---

[443] Empousae are not the only kind of female ghosts. Equally frightening is Lamia. She was a beautiful woman, envied by Hera and turned into an ugly faced monster with the added peculiarity of removable eyes, who snatched or devoured children. Cf. Aristophanes' *Wasps* 1035, *Knights* 693, *Peace* 657; Diodorus 20.41.3; Strabo 1.2.8. For details see Aguirre Castro (1997) 213-224.

Dionysus: Like what?
Xanthias: A terrible one! It takes various forms.
Sometimes it becomes an ox, now it is a mule,
at times it is a beautiful woman.   290
Dionysus:Where? I will throw myself upon her.
Xanthias: But she is woman no more, but a bitch.
Dionysus:Well, then, she is the Empousa.
Xanthias:Her whole face is blazed with fire.
Dionysus:And she has bronze feet?
Xanthias: Yes, by Poseidon; one of them is made of dung.   295
Know this well.[444]

The terrible entity which transforms from bull to mule and then to a beautiful woman and finally to a dog – all common animal forms – turns into a monster with a blazing face, with one copper leg and one made of cow's dung. Of course, one must allow for the comic exaggeration of the monster, but it seems that the hideous form was further enhanced by Aristophanes in other comedies, too. In his *Ecclesiazusae*, a young man describes an amorous old woman who tries to seduce him as 'an Empousa with a body covered with blemishes and blotches'.[445] Whether the skin characteristics are these of the Empousa or of the old woman, is not clear from the text.

According to the 10th c. A.D. lexicon *Suda*, she was 'a phantasma daimonios (demonic ghost) sent by Hecate[446] and would appear to the ill-fated. [Something] which seems to change into many forms. [It is called] Empousa from the fact that it moves on one leg (heni podizein), i.e. that its other leg is bronze. Or because it used to appear from dark places to the initiated. She was also called Oinopole. But others say [that it bore this name] because it changed form. It also seems to appear

---

[444] Aristophanes, Frogs 285-296 (transl. Syropoulos).
[445] Aristophanes, Ecclesiazusae, 1057.
[446] Hecate was the only child of the Titans Perses and Asteria. She was associated with magic, the moon, night, ghosts and necromancy. She was worshipped as a goddess and her cult is associated with the aversion of malignant powers. Her most famous rites were celebrated at Eleusis and the island of Samothrace. She is usually depicted either as a woman holding two torches or three women standing back to back and facing three different directions; this is probably why she is considered to be a goddess of crossroads, which are associated with decision making or turning points in life. As such she is known as Hecate Trimorphis (of three forms). Cf. Pindar, Paean 2. For household shrines to avert evil cf. Aeschylus, fragment 216; Euripides, Medea, 396 ff.; Aristophanes, Ploutos, 410 ff., Wasps, 804 ff.; for shrines at crossroads cf. Aristophanes, Frogs 440 ff.; Pausanias, Description of Greece, 2.30.2; Virgil, Aeneid, 4.609 ff.

in the light of day, when they are offering sacrifices to the dead. Some say that she is the same as Hekate. But [another name for her is] Onokole, because she has an ass' leg; which they call manure (bolitinon), that is donkey manure. For bolitos [is] the proper word for donkey excrement. Aristophanes in *Frogs* [says]: 'by Zeus, I see a huge wild beast.--What kind?--Terrible. It appears to be everywhere at once: at times it is a cow, then a mule, then again a most beautiful woman.--Where is she? I'm heading towards her.--She is no longer a woman, but a dog now.--It is Empousa, then.--At any rate the whole face is glowing with fire and she has a bronze leg.'[447]

Later tradition had it that an Empousa was stalking travelers on the road, however it could be thwarted by verbal abuse. According to Philostratus (1st -2nd c. A.D.) Apollonius of Tyana and his disciple Damis were walking across Mount Caucasus. The night was bright because of the moon, and these were the right circumstances for an appearance of Empousa:

> *While they were travelling by bright moonlight, the ghost of Empousa appeared, once in this form, once in another and at times vanishing completely. Apollonius knew what this was about, and he himself started abusing Empousa verbally and ordered his companions to do the same, because this is, he said, the remedy for such an attack; and the ghost (φάσμα) ran away and disappeared in shrieks, as ghosts always do.*[448]

Three centuries later, Eusebius in his *Treatise Against Hierocles* refers to this incident, simply verifying that the only way to scare off such a monstrous female, was to abuse it by words:

> *He [Philostratus relates how] Apollonios and his companions saw [in Persia on their way to India] some sort of Daemon, to which he gives the name Empousa, along the road, and of how they drove it away by dint of abuse and bad words.*[449]

Eurynomus (Εὐρύνομος)

In the 2nd c. A.D., the Greek travel-writer Pausanias visited the temple of Apollo at Delphi. There he saw a painting of the Underworld by a 5th c. B.C. painter called Polygnotus. Apparently, on it there was the depiction of Eurynomus, a daemon of the underworld, who represented the decay of corpses.[450]

---

[447] Suidas, s.v. Empousa (transl. Suda On Line).
[448] Philostratus, Life of Apollonius of Tyana 2.4 (transl. Syropoulos).
[449] Eusebius, Treatise Against Hierocles, 13 (transl. Jones).
[450] Pausanias, 10.28.7.1-10.28.8.1.

According to the above description, 'Eurynomos, said by the Delphian guides to be one of the daimones of Hades, who eats off all the flesh of the corpses, leaving only their bones. But Homer's Odyssey, the poem called the Minyad, and the Returns, although they tell of Haides and its horrors, know of no Daimon called Eurynomos. However, I will describe what he is like and his attitude in the painting. He is of a color between blue and black, like that of meat flies; he is showing his teeth and is seated, and under him is spread a vulture's skin.'[451]

Gello (Γελλώ)

Just like Empousa, Gello is one of these female monsters used to scare little children. 'When Greek women invoked such terrifying stories, their aim was usually to seek to control unruly children by conjuring up an image of what might happen if they continued to misbehave (a motive explicitly mentioned in our sources).[452]

Gello was believed to snatch little babies, but she could not harm them after they had become one year old, because then they were protected by the fate Adrastos. She was originally a young woman who died at childbirth and was turned into a monster that took babies, especially when they laughed (γελώ means *to laugh*); so, if one saw a baby laugh in its sleep, one ought to wake it up, lest the sound of its laughter drew the attention of Gello.

Sappho, the lyric poetess from Lesbos, commemorated Gello in the phrase Γέλλως παιδοφιλωτέρα, which means *the one who loves children more than Gello*. It was a sarcastic comment about one of her erotic rivals.

Lamia (Λάμια)

Like many other monstrous females, Lamia was formerly an attractive girl. Pausanias tells us that her father was Poseidon and another tradition claims her paternity from the Libyan Belus.[453] Diodorus Siculus (1st c. B.C.) gives us the most complete description of this monster that was exploited in the same sense in which a scary witch or a bogey-woman is utilized today.[454]

Diodorus preserves a very old version of the myth, according to which Lamia, who now lives in the land of Libya, was once a beautiful queen, but each one of her children died at childbirth. Jealous of other women, she turned into a monster. She

---

[451] Pausanias 10.28. 7 (transl. Jones).
[452] Buxton (1994) 18-19. Also n. 6 from Buxton (1994) 19: X. HG 4.4.17, Theoc. 15.40, Str. 1.2.8, schol. Aristid. Or. 102, 5 (vol. III, p. 42 Dindorf).
[453] Pausanias 10.12.2. Cf. Stesichorus Frag. 220.
[454] Diodorus Siculus, Bibliotheca Historica 20.41.3.1-20.42.1.1.

snatched the children of other women and ate them. Her monstrosity is enhanced by the fact that she could take out her own eyes, every time she went to sleep. Diodorus preserves some lines from a play of Euripides, where a character of the play mentions in pity the unfortunate name of Lamia from the land of Libya.

According to other versions, her children were killed by Hera, who was jealous of Zeus' love for Lamia.[455]

Nurses used to force little children to go to sleep by scaring them with the name of Lamia.

Comedy of the 5th c. B.C., especially Aristophanes, was fascinated by the image of Lamia. In his *Wasps,* he exaggerates the form of the monster by adding to it androgynous characteristics, such as ... male genitalia: *unwashed testicles of Lamia.*[456] This joke is repeated in another of his comedies, *Peace*. Again making fun of his hated adversary Cleon, the general of Athenian democracy, Aristophanes describes him as a hideous monster 'shark-toothed, with terrible lightning from his eyes, a hundred heads around him of people who flattered him – if only they would mourn him – licking him, with the voice of a stream that gives birth to havoc, with the stench of a seal, the testicles of a Lamia and the ass of a camel'.[457] Of course, Aristophanes' comic exaggeration should not be taken too seriously. However, Lamia remained a popular monster, which later writers, such as Eustathius, considered to be the mother of the Homeric Scylla.[458]

A more sinister side of Lamia is described by Flavius Philostratus in his *Life of Apollonius of Tyana*.[459] This Lamia uses her seductive powers to lure young men into her cave and she then feasts on their flesh.[460]

Mormo-Mormolyce (Μορμώ- Μορμολύκη)

Mormo means *Frightful*. She is of the same terrible line as Gello and Lamia. An anonymous scholiast on Theocritus' 15.40 equated her with the last two. From this source, we are informed that she was a queen of the Laestrygones, who lost her own children and tried to kill those of others.

---

[455] Buxton (1994) 18; March (2014) 281.
[456] Aristophanes, Wasps 1035.
[457] Aristophanes, Peace 754-759.
[458] Eustathius, Scholia ad Homerum, 1714.
[459] Philostratus, Life of Apollonius 4.25-50-67
[460] For the flesh eating Lamia, see Scholiast on Aristophanes, Peace 758; Dio Chrysostomus, Or. 5; Philostratus, Life of Apollonius 4.25.

Aristophanes mentions her again, as a kind of scary monster, in his *Acharnians:*

'Your terrifying armor makes me dizzy. I beg you, take away that Mormo (bogey-monster)!'[461]

Mormo comes up again in his *Peace:*

'This is terrible! You are in the way, sitting there. We have no use for your Mormo's (bogey-like) head, friend.'[462]

Later, it is Plato who uses the term *Mormolyce* to describe what seems to be the same monster: 'Children are frightened with bogeys (*mormolyttomai*).'[463] The same is found in another one of his dialogues, *Phaedo* 77e:'Try to persuade him not to fear death as if it were a Mormolykeion.'

By the 1st c. B.C. the orator Cicero was wandering 'Where can you find an old wife senseless enough to be afraid of the monsters of the lower world [presumably Empousai, et al] that were once believed in? The years obliterate the inventions of the imagination, but confirm the judgements of nature'.[464] And Strabo, around the end of the 1st c. B.C. and the beginning of the 1st c. A.D. wrote:

And since mythical narrations with monsters do not cause only pleasure, but they also cause fear, the use of both of these genres, myths and stories with monsters, are useful both for children and for adults; for we offer the delightful myths to children in order to urge them towards good, the scary ones in order to avert them from evildoing; because Lamia is a myth and Gorgo and Ephialtes and Mormolyce.[465]

Telchines (Τελχίνες)

Stories about the origins of indigenous inhabitants of every land were traditionally blended with the imaginary, since lack of written sources allowed room for imagination. In the first century A.D., Diodorus of Sicily composed an ambitious account of a 'world history', ranging from the mythical era to 60 B.C. In his fifth book of his *Library of History* he wrote about the island of Rhodes, which was inhabited by a strange race of people called Telchines. They were craftsmen and

---

[461] Aristophanes, Acharnians 582 ff.
[462] Aristophanes, Peace 474 ff.
[463] Plato, Crito 46c.
[464] Cicero, De Natura Deorum, 2.2 (transl. Rackham).
[465] Strabo, Geographica 1.2.8.20-25 (transl. Syropoulos).

wizards, as well as being secretive about their arts, with the added ability to control the weather. These people were also shape-shifters:
55 1 The island which is called Rhodes was first inhabited by the people who were known as Telchines; these were children of Thalatta [i.e. the Sea] as the mythical tradition tells us, and the myth relates that they, together with Capheira, the daughter of Oceanus, nurtured Poseidon, whom Rhea had committed as a babe to their care. 2 And we are told that they were also the discoverers of certain arts and that they introduced other things which are useful for the life of mankind. They were also the first, men say, to fashion statues of gods, and some of the ancient images of gods have been named after them; so, for example, among the Lindians there is an ‹Apollo Telchinius,› as it is called, among the Ialysians a Hera and Nymphae, both called ‹Telchinian,› and among the Cameirans a ‹Hera Telchinia.› 3 And men say that the Telchines were also wizards and could summon clouds and rain and hail at their will and likewise could even bring snow; these things, the accounts tell us, they could do even as could the Magi of Persia; and they could also change their natural shapes and were jealous of teaching their arts to others.
4 Poseidon, the myth continues, when he had grown to manhood, became enamored of Halia, the sister of the Telchines, and lying with her he begat six male children and one daughter, called Rhodos, after whom the island was named.
56 1 At a later time, the myth continues, the Telchines, perceiving in advance the flood that was going to come, forsook the island and were scattered. Of their number Lycus went to Lycia and dedicated there beside the Xanthus river a temple of Apollo Lycius.2 And when the flood came the rest of the inhabitants perished, — and since the waters, because of the abundant rains, overflowed the island, its level parts were turned into stagnant pools — but a few fled for refuge to the upper regions of the island and were saved, the sons of Zeus being among their number. 3 Helius, the myth tells us, becoming enamoured of Rhodos, named the island Rhodes after her and caused the water which had overflowed it to disappear. But the true explanation is *that, while in the first forming of the world the island was still like mud and soft, the sun dried up the larger part of its wetness and filled the land with living creatures, and there came into being the Heliadae, who were named after him, seven in number, and other peoples who were, like them, sprung from the land itself.* 4 In consequence of these events the island was considered to be sacred to Helius, and the Rhodians of later times made it their practice to honor Helius above all the other gods, as the ancestor and founder from whom they were descended. 5 His seven sons were Ochimus, Cercaphus, Macar, Actis, Tenages, Triopas, and Candalus, and there was one daughter, Electryonê, who quit this life while still a maiden and attained at the hands of the Rhodians to honors like those accorded to the heroes. And when the Heliadae attained to manhood they were told by Helius that

the first people to offer sacrifices to Athena would ever enjoy the presence of the goddess; and the same thing, we are told, was disclosed by him to the inhabitants of Attica. 6 Consequently, men say, the Heliadae, forgetting in their haste to put fire beneath the victims, nevertheless laid them on the altars at the time, whereas Cecrops, who was king at the time of the Athenians, performed the sacrifice over fire, but later than the Heliadae. 7 This is the reason, men say, why the peculiar practice as regards the manner of sacrificing persists in Rhodes to this day, and why the goddess has her seat on the island.[466]

Diodorus and Nonnus believe that the Telchines were descendants of the Thalassa, the Sea, and Poseidon.[467] Perhaps this is the reason why Eustathius describes them as marine entities without feet, with fins instead of hands. Eustathius, however, also suggests that they were formerly the dogs of the hunter Actaeon, that were transformed into men – hence their savage nature.[468] Pausanias (2nd c. A.D.) describes a temple of Athena Telchinia in Teumessos in Boeotia. This 'may reflect a tradition of Telchines in the area that would justify their emergence on the slopes of Mount Kithaeron, where Aktaion's dogs turned on their owner'.[469] More names are recorded by Hesychius of Alexandria (5th c. A.D.), such as Mylas. In the 6th c. A.D., Stephanus of Byzantium in his geographical dictionary *Ethnica*, mentions the Telchin Attavyrius, when he talks about Attavyrus, the highest mountain of the island Rhodes. John Tzetzes (c. 1110-1180, Byzantine poet and grammarian) names Megalesius, Antaeus, Hormenus, Lycus, Nicon and Simon.[470]

In a fragment (fr. 93) of some work of the lyric poet Stesichorus (c. 640 – 555 BC) preserved in Eustathius' *ad Iliadem* (772.3), the Telchines are called σκοτώσεις. 'The term is problematic and it could be translated 'shadowy', 'blinded', or 'darkened'. Herter 1934 proposes it may refer to 'the Telchines who cover their eyes' reflecting their possession of the evil eye: the fact that the Stesichoros fragment is preserved in Eustathius in the context of a discussion of jealousy, recommends the hypothesis'.[471]

---

[466] Diodorus, Library, 5. 55.1-5 (transl. Oldfather).
[467] Diodorus. Library 5. 55; Nonnus, Dionysiaca. xiv. 40.
[468] Eustathius, Scholia ad Homerum, p. 771.
[469] Blakely (2007) 265, n. 93.
[470] Tzetzes, Myriobyblos vii. 124, & c.,xii. 835. The full title of Myriobyblos is 'Ιωάννου του Τζέτζου βιβλίον ιστορικόν το δια στίχων πολιτικών, άλφα καλούμενον, ων στίχων το ποσόν μυριάς μια και δισχίλιοι επτακόσιοι πεντήκονταεννέα'. It was turned into Myriobyblos (book of one thousand verses), because of a later editor who divided it in sections constituted of one thousand verses each.
[471] Blakely (2007)265, n. 93.

The Latin poet Ovid considers them daemons, with the power of the 'evil eye', who harmed people. In the 7th book of the *Metamorphoses* he relates the story of Medea's flight to Athens.

> She flew over Astypalaea, the city of Eurypylus, where the women of the island of Cos acquired horns when they abused Hercules, as he and his company departed: over Rhodes, beloved of Phoebus: and the Telchines of the city of Ialysos on Rhodes, whose eyes corrupted everything they looked on, so that Jupiter, disgusted with them, sank them under his brother's ocean waves. She passed the walls of ancient Carthaea, on the island of Ceos, where Alcidamas, as a father, would marvel, one day, that a peace-loving dove could spring from the body of his daughter, Ctesylla.[472]

According to this version, it was Zeus who destroyed them because of their evil nature. 'They also had malevolent powers: they killed animals and plants with a mixture of sulphur and water from the river Styx'.[473] In the Suidas lexicon (10th c. A.D.) under the entry *Telchines* we read:

> [The name of] wicked spirits. Or spiteful and malign humans.[1]
> There were two Telchines, Simon and Nikon. But Nikon was the stronger and obliterated mention of Simon.[2] And [there is] a proverb: 'I know Simon and Simon [knows] me'. In reference to people recognizing evil in each other.[3]
> Also [sc. attested is the adjective] Τελχίνειος .[474]

Epilogue

Why do myths change? In the Introduction of this book, it has been suggested that aspects of politics and localization were notable parameters in the process of giving to myths a different version in different circumstances. Already in the 5th c. B.C. Pherecydes and Hellanicus incorporate in their works mythical traditions regarding exceptional genealogies or foundation myths about their city. No one can be certain about the degree of change in these records, but one cannot rule it out. Myth became too popular and too functional to be ignored. Later *mythographers*, such as Apollodorus, or Hyginus, or even Diodorus, re-collected these traditional narratives and recorded them anew, sometimes referring to non-systematically recorded sources. But, as stressed by Marcel Detienne in his *Mythes grecs et analyse structurale*, in any new literary version, there is never a primal state of a myth

---

[472] Ovid, Metamorphoses, VII, 350-403 (transl.Kline)
[473] March (2014) 459.
[474] Suda online: Byzantine Lexicography, Telchines (http://www.stoa.org/sol).

clearly defined. There is no such thing as an *original myth*, even in the oral tradition of what we call *primitive people*.[475]

Another obvious reason behind the changes in given myth is time. The stories that emerge from an a-temporal, non-chronological *past* evolve, reshape themselves in different historical periods. We have inherited stories that remained popular from the 8th c. B.C. to the 11th c. A.D. But we detect small or great additions, omissions, alterations that do not affect the general outline of a narrative, however, readjust it to a more 'contemporary' version; a version that is more interesting or more easily perceived by its contemporary audience or reader.

This leads us to what should probably be the key parameter to the investigation behind the dynamics of a myth's evolution. Alongside the endogenous causes that allow differentiation of the literary myth, another reason, external this time, plays a key-role in this: it is the audience the writer addressed, which is the recipient of the inherent message conveyed by these stories. Therefore, to the question 'why do myths change?' besides everything else that has been previously suggested, we should add the following: because the audience changes; and the audience, we, the readers, are the only ones qualified to give meaning and worth to the literary message emanating from Mythology.[476]

---

[475] Vernant (2003) 217.
[476] Jauss (1978) 210-62.

Works Cited

A number of secondary sources are referred to in this book. In the case of use of translations, the date indicated in the references is that of the translation's edition. In this section, the full title of the translation is given in the language used and it is followed by the original title and date of the first publication.

Aguirre Castro, Mercedes, Pilar González Serrano-Mercedes Aguirre Castro 'Espíritus malignos, dragones y lamias', ΠΙΟ ΚΟΝΤΑ ΣΤΗΝ ΕΛΛΑΔΑ *(MAS CERCA DE GRECIA)* 12-13 (1997) 213-224.

Aguirre Castro, Mercedes, 'Monstruos y Mitos: las Gorgonas en el Mediterráneo' Revista de Arqueología 207 (1998) 22-31.

Aguirre Castro, Mercedes, 'Monstruos y Mitos: Polifemo el Cíclope' Revista de Arqueología 214 (1999) 14-22.

Aguirre Castro, Mercedes, 'Scylla: hideous monster or femme fatale? A case of contradiction between literary and artistic evidence' Cuadernos de Filología Clásica EGI 12 (2002) 319-328. Articulo citado en A.Bernabé, J. Perez de Tudela, Seres hibridos en la mitología griega, Madrid, Circulo de Bellas Artes 2012.

Aguirre Castro, Mercedes, 'Fantasmas trágicos: algunas observaciones sobre su papel, aparición en escena e iconografía Estudios Griegos e Indoeuropeos 16 (2006) 107-120.

Amayor O. K., ‹Did Herodotus ever go to Egypt?›, Journal of the American Research Center in Egypt, Vol. 15 (1978) 59-73.

Anderson, Graham, Philostratus. Biography and Belles Lettres in the Third Century A.D., London 1986.

Austin Nor., Meaning and Being in Myth, University Park and London, 1990.

Barasch, Moshe, 'The Departing Soul. The Long Life of a Medieval Creation', Artibus et Historiae (IRSA s.c.) 26 (2005) (52): 13–28.

Bauer, S. Wise, The History of the Ancient World, W.W. Norton & Company, New York (2007).

Bell, E. Robert, Women of Classical Mythology: A Biographical Dictionary, ABC-CLIO 1991.

Blakely, Sandra, Myth, Ritual and Metallurgy in Ancient Greece and Recent Africa, Cambridge University Press, Cambridge 2007.

Bolton, J. D. P., Aristeas of Proconnesus (Oxford: Clarendon Press, 1962;reprinted 1992)

Bowden, Hugh. Mystery Cults of the Ancient World, Princeton University Press, 2010.

Bowie, E. L., 'Apollonius of Tyana: Tradition and Reality', ANRW 2, no. 16, 2 (1978) pp. 1663-1667.

Bowie, Ewen and Jaś Elsner (eds.). *Philostratus. Greek culture in the Roman world*, Cambridge; New York: Cambridge University Press, 2009.
Bremmer, Jan, *Interpretations of Greek Mythology*, Routledge Revivals, 2013 (original edition 1987).
Burkert, Walter, 'Oriental and Greek Mythology: The Meeting of Parallels', in Jan Bremmer (Ed.) *Interpetations of Greek Mythology*, 2013 (original edition 1987) 10-40.
Burkert, Walter, *Ancient Mystery Cults*, Harvard University Press, 1987.
Bury, John Bagnell, *The Ancient Greek Historians*, Dover Publications, New York, 1958.
Buxton, Richard, G. A., *Imaginary Greece, the Contexts of Mythology*, Cambridge 1996 3rd editon (original edition 1994).
Buxton, Richard, G. A., 'Wolves and Werewolves in Greek Thought', in Jan Bremmer (Ed.) *Interpetations of Greek Mythology*, 2013 (original edition 1987) 60-79.
Buxton, Richard, G. A., *The Complete World of Greek Mythology*, Thames & Hudson, 2004.
Cameron, Alan, *Greek Mythography in the Roman World*, OUP USA 2004.
Campbell, Joseph, *The Hero with a Thousand Faces*, 1949.
Campbell, Joseph, *The Masks of God*, Vol. 3: Occidental Mythology. Penguin Books, 1968.
Carpenter, T.H., *Art and Myth in Ancient Greece*, London, 1991
Carter, D. M., *The Politics of Greek Tragedy*, Bristol Phoenix Press, 2007.
Casson, S., 'The Hyperboreans', *The Classical Review* 34.1/2 (February - March 1920) 1–3.
Cheremisin, D. V. & Zaporozhchenko, A. V. 'The 'Sacred Centres' of Eurasia and the Legend about the Arimaspi and the Griffins', Barnaul, 1999.
Dennys, Rodney, *The Heraldic Imagination*, Barrie & Jenkins, London, 1975.
Detienne, Marcel, *The Writings of Orpheus. Greek Myth in Cultural Context*, translated by Janet Lloyd, Johns Hopkins University Press, 2003 [originally published as *L' Écriture d' Orphée*, Editions Galimmard, 1989].
Doniger, Wendy, *The Implied Spider. Politics and Theology in Myth*, Columbia University Press, 2011.
Dowden, Ken, *The Uses of Greek Mythology*, Routledge, London 1992, 2005 (second edition).
Dzielska, Maria, *Apollonius of Tyana in Legend and History*, Rome 1986.
Easterling, P. E. & Muir, J. V., *Greek Religion and Society*, Cambridge University Press, Cambridge, 1993 (5th edition, original edition: 1985).
Erickson, Gerald, *Possesssion, Sex and Hysteria: The Growth of Demonism in Later Antiquity*, in Fred E. H. Schroeder, *5000 years of popular culture: popular culture before printing*, Green State University Popular Press, 1980, 109-136.

Farkas, A. E., Harper, P. O. & Harrison, E. B. (eds.), *Monsters and Demons in the Ancient and Medieval Worlds: Papers Presented in Honour of Edith Porada*, Mainz am Rhein, von Zabern, 1987.

Finucane, R. C., *Appearances of the Dead: A Cultural History of Ghosts*, Prometheus Books, 1984.

Fuller, John Frederick Charles, *The Generalship of Alexander the Great*, Da Capo Press, 2004.

Flinterman, Jaap-Jan, *Power, Paideia and Pythagoreanism*, Amsterdam 1995.

Gantz, Timothy, *Early Greek Myth: A Guide to Literary and Artistic Sources*, Johns Hopkins University Press, 1996 (Vol. 1).

Goldhill, S. & Osborne, R. (eds), *Art and Text in Ancient Greek Culture. (Cambridge Studies in New Art History and Criticism)*. Cambridge University Press, Cambridge 1994.

Gould, C., B.A., *Myhical Monsters*, Electronical Reprint by Arment Bilogical Press, 2000 (originally published by W. H. Allen & Co. in London in 1886).

Gow, A. S. F. & Scofield A. F., *Nicander: The Poems and Poetical Fragments*, 1953.

Graves, Robert, *The Greek Myths*, The Folio Society, London 1996 [here utilized the 13th printing in two volumes, 2002].

Graziosi, Barbara, *The Invention of Homer*, Cambridge, 2002.

Grimal, Pierre. *The Dictionary of Classical Mythology*. NY: Blackwell Reference, 1986.

Guthrie, W. K. C., *The Greeks and their Gods*, Beacon Press, Boston 2001, first edition in 1950.

Guthrie, W. K. C., *Orpheus and Greek Religion*, Methuen & Co. Ltd, London (1952) [here used the Greek translation by Charikleia Mene, Kardamitsa editions, Athens 2000].

Hammond, Nicholas, G. L. 'Cavalry recruited in Macedonia down to 322 B.C.', *Historia: Zeitschrift für Alte Geschichte* 47 (4th quarter of 1998) 404–425.

Hansen, William, *Handbook of Classical Mythology*, ABC-CLIO, 2004.

Hard, Robin, *The Routledge Handbook of Greek Mythology: Based on H.J. Rose's 'Handbook of Greek Mythology'*, Psychology Press, 2004.

Hopkinson, Neil, (ed.), *Lucian: A Selection. Cambridge Greek and Latin Texts*. Cambridge/New York: Cambridge University Press, 2008.

Hopman, Marianne Govers, *Scylla: Myth, Metaphor, Paradox*, Cambridge University Press, 2013.

Jauss H.R., *Pour une esthétique de la réception* tr.fr. par Cl., Paris : Gallimard, 1978.

Jacoby, Felix, *Atthis: The Local Chronicles of Ancient Athens*, Ayer Co. Pub., new edition, June 1949.

Johnson, Michael & Sharwood Smith, John, *The Greeks and their Myths. The classic stories with their origins and meanings*, Eurobook Limited, 1992.

Kerényi, Karl, Η Μυθολογία των Ελλήνων, Εστία Press, Athens 1982, 2nd edition (transl. by Δημήτρης Σταθόπουλος). Originally published as *Die Mythologie der Griechen*, 1966.
Knoefel, P., K. & Covi M. C., *A Hellenistic Treatise on Poisonous Animals (The 'Theriaca' of Nicander of Colophon): A Contribution to the History of Toxicology*, 1991.
Kirk, G., S., *The Nature of Greek Myths*, 1975.
Lefkowitz, Mary, *Greek Gods, Human lives. What We Can Learn from Myths*, Yale University Press, 2003 [here utilized the translation in Greek by Alexandra Melista, Θνητοί και Αθάνατοι. Οι θεοί των αρχαίων Ελλήνων και ο ρόλος τους στη ζωή των ανθρώπων, Μεταίχμιο, Athens, 2005].
Lendon, J. E., *Soldiers and Ghosts: A history of Battle in Classical Antiquity*, Yale University Press 2006.
Lévi-Strauss, Claude, Μύθος και νόημα, transl. Vagelis Athanasopoulos, Kardamitsa, Athens, 1986 (original publication, 1978).
Lonsdale, David, J., *Alexander the Great: lessons in strategy*, Routledge 2007.
Malinowski Bruno., *Myth in primitive psychology*, London, 1926.
March, Jenny, *Dictionary of Classical Mythology*, Oxbow Books, 2014 (first edition 1998).
Mariolakos, I., 'The Geomythological Geotopes of Lerni Springs (Argolis, Greece)', *Geologica Balcanica* 28 (1998) 3-4, 101-108.
Mayor, Adrienne, 'A triton pulled my leg! Greek mermaids and sea monsters', *The Athenian* (September 1985) 21-24
Mayor, Adrienne & Heaney, Michael, 'Griffins and Arimaspeans', *Folklore* Vol. 104, No 1/2 (1993) 40-66.
Morford, Mark, P.O. & Lenardon, Robert, J., *Classical Mythology* (7th edition), Oxford University Press, New York & Oxford, 2003.
Müller, Gottfried, *Isaakiou kai Ioannou tou Tzetzou Scholia eis Lykophrona* [ΣΧΟΛΙΑ ΕΙΣ ΛΥΚΟΦΡΟΝΑ], Vol. 3, Leiden, 1811.
Myres, J. L., 'The wanderings of Io: Aeschylus, *Prometheus* 707-869', *The Classical Review* 60. 1 (April 1946) 2-4.
Narby, J., *The Cosmic Serpent: DNA and the origins of Knowledge*, Jeremy P.Tarcher/Putnam editions, New York 1999.
Oberhelman, Steve, 'Greek and Roman Witches', in in Fred E. H. Schroeder, *5000 years of popular culture: popular culture before printing*, Green State University Popular Press, 1980, 137-154.
Ogden, Daniel, *Drakon. Dragon Myth and Serpent Cult in the Greek and Roman Worlds*, Oxford University Press, 2013.
Price, Robert, M., *The Christ-Myth Theory and its Problems*, Atheist Press, 2011.
Regier, Willis Goth, *Book of the Sphinx*, Univeristy of Nebraska Press, Lincoln 2004.
Sabin, Frances E. *Classical Myths That Live Today*. NY: Silver Burdett Company, 1940.

Sallares, R., *The ecology of the ancient Greek world*, Cornell University Press, 1991.
Scott, Alan 'The Date of the Physiologus' *Vigiliae Christianae* 52.4 (November 1998) 430-441).
Scott, Leonard & McClure Michael, *Myth and Knowing: An Introduction to World Mythology*, Boston, McGraw Hill, 2004.
Shotwell, James, T., *The History of History*, Columbia University Press, New York, 1939.
Spense, Lewis, *The Myths of the North American Indians*, London: George G. Harrap & Co, 1914
Spyridakis, S., 'Zeus is Dead: Euhemerus and Crete', *CJ*, Vol. 63, No. 8 (May 1968) 337-340.
Stockstad, Marilyn & Cothren, Michael W., *Art History*, Prentice Hall, 2011.
Struck, Peter, T., *Birth of the Symbol' Ancient Readers at the Limits of their Texts*, Princeton University Press, Princeton 2004.
Symeonides, N. K.; et al. (2001). 'New data on Palaeoloxodon chaniensis (Vamos cave, Chania, Crete)'. In Cavarretta, Giuseppe (ed.), *The World of Elephants - International Congress, Rome 2001*, Rome 2001, 510-513.
Vernant, Jean-Pierre, *Myth et société en Grèce ancienne*, La Découverte, 1974 [here utilized the translation in Greek by Katerina Alexopoulou & Spyros Georgakopoulos, Μεταίχμιο, 2005].
Vernant, Jean-Pierre et Vidal-Naquet, Pierre, *Mythe et tragédie en Grèce ancienne* (tome 2), Maspero, 172 (rééd. La Découverte, 1986).
Vernant, Jean-Pierre et Vidal-Naquet, Pierre, *La Grèce ancienne, t. 1 : Du mythe à la raison et t. 2 : Rites de passages et trangression*, Seuil.
Versnel, H. S., *Inconsistencies in Greek and Roman Religion: Transition and Reversal in Myth and Ritual* (Studies in Greek and Roman Religion, v. 6) Brill, 1993.
Veyne, Paul, *Did the Greeks Believe in their Myths? An Essay on the Constituive Imagination*, The University of Chicago Press, Chicago and London 1988 (transl. by Paula Wissing). Originally published as *Les Grecs ont-ils cru à leurs mythes?* Editions du Seuil, 1983.
Walter, Katie, *Reading Skin in Medieval Literature and Culture*, Palgrave Macmillan, 2013.
Waters, K. H.,. *Herodotos the Historian: His Problems, Methods, and Originality*. Norman, University of Oklahoma Press, 1985. Introduction.
White, T. H., *The Bestiary: The Book of Beasts*, London & New York, 1954, 1960 (4th edition).
Woodard, Roger (ed.), *The Cambridge Companion to Greek Mythology*, Cambridge 2007.
Yamaguchi, Nobuyuki; Cooper, Alan; Werdelin, Lars; MacDonald, David W. (2004). ‹Evolution of the mane and group-living in the lion (*Panthera leo*): a review'. *Journal of Zoology* 263 (4): 329.

Greek

Βεικος Θ., *Ο μύθος του λόγου*, Αθήνα, Παπαζήσης, 1977.
Κακριδής, Ι., *Ελληνική Μυθολογία*, Αθήνα, 1986
Καρακάντζα, Ε. Δ., *Αρχαίοι Ελληνικοί Μύθοι. Ο θεωρητικός λόγος του 20ου αιώνα για τη φύση και την ερμηνεία τους*, Μεταίχμιο 2004.
Συρόπουλος, Σ., ‹Σκηνική Νεκρομαντεία και Αθηναϊκή Πολιτική: η Νεκρανάσταση του Δαρείου στους Πέρσες του Αισχύλου και η Ιστορική Συνείδηση› [‹Stage Necromancy and Athenian Politics: the Resurrection of Darius in Aeschylus' *Persians* and Historical Consciousness'] στο *Θέατρο και Πόλη. Αττικό Δράμα, Αθηναϊκή Δημοκρατία και Αρχαία Ελληνική Θρησκεία*, επιμ. Α. Μαρκαντωνάτος & Λ. Πλατυπόδης, Gutenberg, Αθήνα 2012, 83-105.

Ancient Greek Sources – Translations and Commentaries (English)

Aelian, *On the Nature of Animals*. Translated by Gregory McNamee. 2011. Trinity University Press.
Aelian, *Historical Miscellany*. Translated by Nigel G. Wilson. 1997. Loeb Classical Library.
Aelian, *On Animals*. 3 volumes. Translated by A. F. Scholfield. 1958-9. Loeb Classical Library.
Aeschylus. Translated by Smyth, Herbert Weir. Loeb Classical Library Volumes 145 & 146. Cambridge, MA. Harvard Universrity Press. 1926.
Apollodorus, *The Library*, with and English Translation by Sir James George Frazer, two volumes, London, New York, 1921.
Apollodorus. *The Library of Greek Mythology*. A new translation by Robin Hard, Oxford University Press, Oxford & New York 2008 (1st edition in 1997).
Apollodorus. *Gods & Heroes of the Greeks. The Library of Apollodorus*. Translated with Introduction and Notes by Michael Simpson, The University of Massachussetts Press, 1976.
Apollonius Rhodius. *The Argonautica*, with and English translation by R. C. Seaton, Harvard University Press, the Loeb Library, 1927.
Claudian. Translated by Platnauer, Maurice. Loeb Classical Library Volumes 135 & 136. Cambridge, MA. Harvard Univserity Press. 1922.
Diodorus Siculus. Diodorus of Sicily in Twelve Volumes with an English Translation by C. H. Oldfather. Vol. 4-8. Cambridge, Mass.: Harvard University Press; London: William Heinemann, Ltd. 1989.
Eustathius. Joann. Aug. Gottl Weigel, *Eustathi Archiepiscopi Thessalonicensis, Commentarii ad Homeri Iliadem*, Vol. 1, Lipsiae 1827.

Euripides. *Euripides, with an English translation by David Kovacs,* Cambridge. Harvard University Press. 1994.
Herodotus, with an English translation by A. D. Godley. Cambridge. Harvard University Press. 1920.
Homer. *The Iliad of Homer,* translated with an introduction by Richmond Lattimore, The University of Chicago Press, Chicago and London, 1961 (original edition 1951).
Homer. *The Odyssey of Homer,* translated with an introduction by Richmond Lattimore, Harper Perennial, 1975 (original edition 1965).
Homeric Hymns. *Homeric Hymns,* translated by Sarah Ruden, with an introduction by Sheila Murnaghan, Hacket Publishing Company, 2005.
Nonnus, *Dionysiaca*. Translated by Rouse, W H D. Loeb Classical Library Volumes 344, 354, 356. Cambridge, MA, Harvard University Press, 1940
Philostratus, *Apollonius of Tyana*. 3 volumes. Translated by Christopher P. Jones. 2005-6. Loeb Classical Library.
Pseudo-Hyginus, *Astronomica* (translated by Mary Grant, in http://www.theoi.com)

Ancient Greek Sources – Translations and Commentaries (Greek)

Παυσανίας. Παυσανίου, Ελλάδος Περιήγησις, Ά Αττικά, μτφ. Δ. Λαμπίκη, εκδ. Πάπυρος, Αθήνα 1975.
Πλούταρχος. Πλουτάρχου, Βίοι Παράλληλοι, Θησεύς, μτφ. Α. Πουρναρά, τόμος 1, εκδ. Πάπυρος, Αθήνα 1975
Στράβων. Στράβωνος Γεωγραφικά, Ζ΄, μτφ. Κ. Θ. Αραπόπουλου, τόμος 3, εκδ. Πάπυρος , Αθήνα 1975

Electronic Sources

Ancient Greek Mythology: http://www.greekmyth.org
http://greekmythology.com
Greek Mythology Link: http://www.maiar.com/GML/
Theoi Greek Mythology: http://www.theoi.com
Electronic Resources for Classicists: http://www.tlg.uci.edu/index/resources.html
Perseus Digital Library: http://www.perseus.tufts.edu/
Suda on Line: http://www.stoa.org/sol/
Cosmic serpents: Nancy C. Maryboy, http://cosmicserpent.org/about-us/the-cosmic-serpent.html
Reliability of Herodotus: http://www.loyno.edu/~history/journal/1998-9/Pipes.htm
Open Library Text Books: https://openlibrary.org/books/OL6637176M/The_library

Encyclopedias

Lexicon Iconographicum Mythologiae Classicae (LIMC), Artemis & Winkler Verlag (Zürich, München, Düsseldorf), Vol. IV: Eros (in Etruria) - Herakles (1988), Vol. V: Herakles - Kenchrias (1990).

Disclaimer

The reproduction of photos included in this book is free of copyright restrictions, as stated by the agent of their web publication, since they belong to the public domain (http://en.wikipedia.org/wiki/Public_domain)
See also: CONSOLIDATED ACT ON COPYRIGHT
http://portal.unesco.org/culture/admin/file_download.php/dk_copyright_2003_en.pdf